# Hiding In A Cave
# Of Trunks

To Janet

with

Best wishes

Ester Shepherd

2013

# What people are saying about *Hiding in a Cave of Trunks*:

The author has done invaluable work to trace the story of her family's century-long existence in Shanghai and provides a vivid sense of Jewish life in wartime Shanghai during Japanese occupation. This is an important contribution to the history of the Jewish experience in China, especially the history of the Sephardi Jewish community in Shanghai. I congratulate her on the appearance of this remarkable work.

**PAN Guang**
Professor and Dean
Center of Jewish Studies Shanghai (CJSS)

The story of the Shanghai Jews is an important part of the history of the world Jewry. *Hiding in a Cave of Trunks* by Ester Benjamin Shifren offers a vivid, fascinating and all-round portrait of the community in war-time Shanghai. Readable, powerful and valuable. Must be read.

**Xu Xin**
Professor and Director of The Glazer Institute of Jewish and Israel Studies, Nanjing University, author of *The Jews of Kaifeng, China: History, Culture, and Religion* (2003)

Ester has brought awareness of the American and European peoples' contribution, in both work and play, to Far Eastern advancement and development in the first half of the 20th Century. Many dedicated their lives to imparting knowledge of the modern world to the people they lived amongst, and with whom they developed a special relationship. It is a "must read" for anyone wanting a balanced view of the times.

**Ron Bridge** MBE, AFC. Ex-internee Weihsien Camp. Chairman, ABCIFER—Association of British Civilian Internees Far East Region.

*Hiding in a Cave of Trunks* is a thoroughly engaging, fast-paced story of Ester's relatives and her wartime and post-war experiences. Combined with that, the lively, fascinating descriptions of Shanghai and Hong Kong street scenes, and unusual information about pre- and post-war China, make this compelling book well worth the journey.

**Margaret Blair**, ex-child internee, author of *Gudao, Lone Islet, The War Years in Shanghai* and *Shanghai Scarlet*

Ester Benjamin Shifren's poignant childhood memories, of experiencing the Holocaust as a British Sephardi Jew from Shanghai, bring out some happy camp experiences as well as the horrors of living in the Yu Yuen Road and Yangtzepoo Camps, and being threatened by the Japanese Commandant toward the end of the Japanese occupation. Much of her childhood was taken away from her due to Japanese imperialism and fascism during WWII, and family members suffered permanent physical damage from their internment. This is Ester's opportunity to voice her experiences for the world to never forget the paradoxical Japanese treatment of POWs and numerous Jews.

Ester and her family have been denied reparations by the British and the Japanese for their three years incarceration. Holocaust museums throughout the world have failed to commemorate her story and that of others amongst the Jewish Diaspora in the Far East during the Holocaust. This is a first in giving an Eastern Jewish perspective of both the Holocaust and pre-WWII history of the Mizrahi Jews of the Far East.

**Professor Yitzchak Kerem**, historian and researcher of Sephardic and Eastern Jewry, and editor of *Sefarad*, the Sephardic Newsletter, The Hebrew University of Jerusalem, and founder of the upcoming Beit Maksim, the Sephardic/Mizrahi Museum and Cultural Arts Center of Jerusalem.

Ester Benjamin Shifren's account of her family's experiences in Shanghai—both before and during the Japanese invasion of China during WWII—makes for gripping reading. Told from her own perspective as a young Jewish girl growing up in a fascinating world where cultures mingle and where age-old traditions define the very fabric of everyday life, she takes us on a journey that is a dazzling testament to courage and the endurance of the human spirit. It is an astonishing story.

**Lionel Friedberg**, New York Times bestselling author and Emmy Award-winning producer

A truly absorbing story of human survival

**Diana Friedberg**, Film Producer and Author

# Hiding in a Cave of Trunks

A Prominent Jewish Family's Century in Shanghai
and Internment in a WWII POW Camp

## Ester Benjamin Shifren

Use of image negative # A30855, by kind written permission from
Yvonne Oliver.
The Imperial War Museum, London, UK.


Cover design: Scott Greene


Front cover photo, Ester age 9, and Ester, HMS Belfast 2005.
Back cover author photo: Dr. Ron Lever

ISBN 978-1479165384
ISBN 1479165387

For my mother, Liza, and in memory of my father, Benjy.

# CONTENTS

THE CARDS OF LIFE

ANCESTRY STRUCTURE

PREFACE

PART ONE: EARLY CHILDHOOD DAYS IN SHANGHAI

The Photograph ................................................1
Early Childhood ................................................7
My Maternal Grandparents................................13
Liza................................................................21
Great-Grandmother Matana .............................27
The Benjamins ................................................31
Mummy Meets Daddy.......................................37
Benjy and Liza's Wedding..................................45
Kidnapped! ......................................................49
The Court Case.................................................53
The Battle for Shanghai.....................................57
Nanking...........................................................63
Auntie Sally .....................................................67
Amah...............................................................71
Mosquito Nets .................................................77
Auntie Eileen ...................................................81
The Zetza Family ..............................................83
Floods in the International Settlement .................85
Hongkew .........................................................89
The Japanese Occupation ..................................97
Daddy Gives Up His Car ..................................101
The Notice.......................................................105
Cakes and Tears ...............................................109


PART TWO: FROM FREEDOM TO CAPTIVITY

Captives..........................................................115
First Days in Camp...........................................121

Making the Best of It .................................................125
Maize and Soybean Milk..........................................131
Hell's Bells .............................................................139
Yangtzepoo Camp....................................................143
Bridge House...........................................................149
Last Days in Camp ..................................................153

PART THREE: HOMECOMING

Homecoming...........................................................161
The *Belfast* Tea Party—1945 ....................................169
Shanghai British School ...........................................175
Chinese New Year ....................................................181
The Minny Family ...................................................185
The Communists .....................................................189

PART FOUR: HONG KONG

Hong Kong..............................................................197
King George V School ..............................................201
New Beginnings.......................................................207
Growing Up.............................................................211
Secret Society Aspirations.........................................215
Nathan Road ...........................................................219
Adolescence ............................................................223
Yip the Gyp ............................................................227
Last Days in China ..................................................231

LONDON 2005: WE'LL MEET AGAIN.............................237
DÉJÀ VU PARTY ON THE *HMS BELFAST* .......................243
AUTHOR'S AFTERWORD ...............................................249
ACKNOWLEDGMENTS .................................................253

# THE CARDS OF LIFE

Life dealt me cards—I played my hand
With confidence—I had it planned…
When, later, life revealed the score
It shook me to my very core!
I wondered then—still wonder now
Could I have changed my life somehow?
And—if life dealt this hand again
Would I repeat my life of pain?
Or would my hand, ignoring me
Repeat this life and destiny?


Ester Benjamin Shifren

# ANCESTRY STRUCTURE

LEVEL 1:
    1.1    Miriam Isaacs (nee David)—great-great grandmother
    1.2    Nuriel Isaacs—great-great grandfather

LEVEL 2:
    2.1    Matana  Nissim (nee Isaacs)—great-grandmother
    2.2    Matook Nissim—great-grandfather

LEVEL 3:
    3.1    Essie Benjamin (nee Nissim)—paternal grandmother
    3.1.1 David Hai Benjamin—paternal grandfather
CHILDREN: Benjy, Leah, Sally, Syd, Eileen, Eva.
    3.2    Yeheskel Jacob Arzooni—maternal grandfather
    3.2.1 Haviva—maternal grandmother
CHILDREN: Isaac, Grace, Victoria, Jack, Liza, Moses, David.

LEVEL 4:
    4.1    Benjamin Frederick Benjamin—father
    4.1.1 Liza Benjamin (nee Jacob Arzooni)—mother

LEVEL 5:
CHILDREN:
    5.1    David Benjamin
    5.2    Ester Shifren (nee Benjamin)
    5.3    Sylvia Lief (nee Benjamin)

FAMILY TREE—FIVE GENERATIONS IN SHANGHAI

Great-great Grandmother Miriam Isaacs

# PREFACE

In the mid 1800s, before there was an official registry of Jewish settlers in China, my paternal great-great-grandparents, Nuriel and Miriam Isaacs, traveled the lengthy journey from Calcutta, India, to Chinkiang, now Zhenjiang, (translated as *River Garrison*), the walled treaty port city in Kiangsu Province, now Jiangsu Province, where the Grand Canal intersects the Yangtze River. They journeyed on a vessel captained by Nuriel, who had regularly traveled the well-beaten trade route. In 1871, their youngest child, my great-grandmother Matana, was born on the junk that housed them in Chinkiang for several years until they relocated to nearby Shanghai.

They were all British subjects, fervently loyal to the Crown, and were amongst the first Jewish migrants to China in that era. They conversed in English and Hindustani, which they had learnt in India. In those early days in Chinkiang, my great-great-grandmother's brother, David Moses David, was appointed Honorary Dutch Consul, and held that office until a replacement was sent from Belgium. Family lore has it that my great-great-grandfather, Nuriel Isaacs, also "held the fort" while a British Consul was away.

On reaching Shanghai they were registered with other prominent Jewish newcomers. Among the best-known names of these early arrivals were the Sassoon, Hardoon and Kadoorie families, who in time amassed great personal wealth, led opulent lifestyles, and contributed greatly to the development and wealth of Shanghai. They had many servants and entertained lavishly in their grandiose homes.

The religiously observant regularly attended synagogue services, and donated generously to charity. They funded the building of schools, hospitals, synagogues and cemeteries, and promoted the richly diversified cultural life of the city. Some had lived in India and Burma, and had business dealings with Shanghai before permanently moving to China. They encouraged family members from Iraq and India to join their business ventures, facilitating their immigration by helping them to settle well in their new homes.

Jewish presence in China occurred hundreds of years earlier, during the eighth and ninth centuries. Persian Jews traveled the silk route from Persia to China and some settled in Kaifeng, at that time a large capital city. They broke their journey to rest on the Sabbath, observing the religious commandment, and built dwellings for others who followed in their footsteps. The newcomers, though adhering to their Judaism, assimilated with the Chinese, largely adopting their culture and habits—including foot binding, a custom started in the 10th century. Ample authentic documentation exists about these early settlers.

More than ten centuries later, I was born the fifth generation of a family who lived and thrived in China for a span of more than one hundred years.

# EARLY CHILDHOOD DAYS IN SHANGHAI

Party on HMS Belfast -- Shanghai 1945

Ester on swing, David on right

# THE PHOTOGRAPH

I'm staring at four photographs covering the front page of the *Bamboo Wireless* bulletin. In one of them—swinging in mid-air—is joyful, widely smiling, eight-year-old me. A pretty ribbon is in my neatly combed, curly hair. I look intently at the children in the other pictures, willing myself to identify them. Who are they? And who took these photos that have emerged more than half a century after the war?

A wave of nostalgia overtakes me when I see the majestic ship. I read the short paragraph:

**CHILDREN'S PARTY SHANGHAI 1ST OCTOBER 1945**
*HMS Belfast* arrived in Shanghai in September 1945 and was involved in relief work concerning British Civilian Internees for the next three months. Now moored in the Thames as part of the Imperial War Museum, they are anxious to contact as many who were at the Party or who had any involvement with the *HMS Belfast*. The plan is to re-create the Party sometime in the summer or early autumn 2005 as part of the "SeaBritain" Festival. Write to Nick Hewitt…

I'm breathless. My hands shake as I dial Nick's number. "I'm Ester Shifren," I say, "the child on the swing."

Nick listens to my story. "I'm delighted to hear from you," he says. "It's wonderful to have an identity. We'd love you to attend. I know it's a long way—any chance of you coming from Los Angeles?"

The prospect is tempting. "Well, I'm definitely going to consider it. How many 'children' have you found?"

"We don't know yet," Nick says, "but we're hoping to locate as many as possible. We want this to be a very special event."

Shortly thereafter, thanks to Nick's referral, I receive a call from Anna Fowler, of BBC One, in London. She asks, "How did it feel to go on board the *Belfast?*"

"It was wonderful—the sailors welcomed us so warmly. They hugged and carried us on their shoulders and played games with us." In recall, my eyes sting with sudden tears. "The smell of the sumptuous food was intoxicating. We all gorged ourselves and suffered happily from stomach aches for days after the party!"

"Can you send me a written description?"

"Sure," I say, and later sent her the following: *I remember going up the gangplank holding Mummy's hand... I could hardly contain my excitement—it was wonderful being at the river, with all the smells that go with it. It was our first experience of freedom after the internment, which was just like being let out of jail. We had all recently been ill with dysentery and other ailments brought on by the harsh conditions in camp...*

Multiple calls and emails later, Anna asks, "Would you consider taking part in our television program? We'll pay all of your expenses."

"Are you kidding me? Shall I swim halfway?" My heart is bursting with excitement!


I'm in London, a guest of BBC One in their show, *We'll Meet Again*, commemorating the 60th anniversary of Victory in Europe (VE) Day. Ours is the second of several highly emotional, meaningful episodes reuniting people who had lost touch after the war.

Dame Vera Lynn, the vocalist who popularized the wartime title-song, is a special guest participant. I feel extremely privileged to be part of the same show!

Ten fellow "children" and I are part of an audience comprised mainly of participants and their families and friends. The excitement is palpable!

Sixty years after the war, BBC One has somehow managed to find three elderly ex-*Belfast* sailors. They're seated onstage, being questioned by popular television personality, Des Lynam. Bright lights accentuate the rather puzzled look on their weathered faces. They have no idea what's in store...

Film-footage of the 1945 party is repeatedly playing on a stage-wide background screen. In one clip I'm swinging back and forth in a makeshift swing, specially rigged up for the occasion on the ship's deck. I look blissfully happy. My mother, brother, and sister are nearby, leaning against the railings.

I watch, transfixed. Suddenly, I'm that young child again—overwhelmed by memories of my stolen early childhood years. My eyes fill with tears.

*Yes*, I think, *I have come a long way—from a far greater distance than Los Angeles*. My mind is swinging back and forth, further and further back, in rhythm with the swinging eight-year-old child on the screen—back in time to a freezing winter's day in January 1942, in Shanghai, China.

Ester sitting second from the right. David is first from left in top row.

I'm so excited! Today is Li-li's first birthday. She's my baby sister, who got her nickname from me when she was born, because it was hard for me to say "Sylvia." I'm four years old, and David is six. He copies me and also calls her Li-li.

Li-li is so cute—with big, beautiful, alert brown eyes that follow us around everywhere. She laughs a lot and loves the games we make up for her amusement. Today she just seems to know it's her own special day. Amah, the term for our Chinese maid, has dressed her in a pretty, lacey white frock that she keeps touching, while making sounds of appreciation as she waddles around carefully on tiptoes, showing off to everyone.

Mummy and Amah made sandwiches and jelly and baked wonderful cakes and cookies for the party, while I sat quietly in the kitchen enjoying the lovely smell of vanilla. Amah gave me a fancy salmon sandwich—it's my favorite! She braided her shining black hair, and looks so nice in her starched white jacket and black silk pants.

All of our cousins are coming to the party. Auntie Sally is bringing

Tony. They're our neighbors and we play with Tony every day. I wish my cousins who live in Hong Kong could also come... We often visit Mummy's brothers' children in the big house they share with Granny and Grandpa. They have a large black cat that's almost as big as I am. He catches all their rats and cockroaches.

Daddy said there's been a lot of loud bombing and shooting going on near the International Settlement, where we live. He and Mummy often talk about the war and the Japanese invasions and cruelty to the Chinese. They call it "atrocities." They fear for the future of Shanghai. Many foreigners already left to live in other countries.

Today no one speaks about the war. Sometimes I become frightened when I hear them talk about the fighting, even though I don't really understand. I always cover my ears when I hear the airplanes and bombs. David isn't scared—he plays war games with his toy soldiers.

It's three o'clock—Magda and Yah-lee have arrived. I love them. They're my best friends and live in our building. We always play together. What fun! They don't go to the synagogue because they're not Jewish, like us. Yah-lee is half Chinese.

We're going to sing "Happy Birthday," and play *Blind Man's Buff* and *Pin the Tail on the Donkey*. Li-li keeps clapping her hands. She's already smeared chocolate on the front of her pretty dress, but nobody minds. It's her special day after all.

I heard Daddy say, "Many Jewish refugees flooded into Shanghai. Their stories are so sad. Many have lost their entire family, because Adolph Hitler is murdering Jews and non-Jews. He's an evil Nazi dictator."

How can you lose your whole family? I can't imagine what that means. No more birthdays—ever again? I'm so happy we're all together today.

Daddy said our Sephardic community, which has lived here for many years, helped the refugees with food and shelter. Some of the newcomers were not feeling very well after their long, difficult journey. Sometimes he and Mummy speak with friends and family about the problem of Shanghai accepting so many people. No one needed papers or visas to come here because it's a "Treaty Port"—whatever that means.

Many Sephardim have British passports. Daddy is so proud of his family being British for so many years, beginning when they lived in British India. Everyone stands to attention whenever they play *God Save the King*—the national anthem.

I wish we had a piano, but we don't have enough money to buy one because times are so difficult now. While Mummy is practicing diving at the YMCA indoor pool, I watch people playing the piano in the recreation hall. I listen carefully, and when they leave I pick out the tunes I remember. I still can't stretch my fingers very far because they're too small.

One day I'm going to be a musician and sing and dance on a stage. That's what I love most. It's my secret dream. I practice on the radiator, pretending it's my piano. Daddy can play all the popular songs by ear and Mummy dances many different styles. There's always a lot of music around us.

I can't wait to see Li-li's presents. Everyone's making a fuss over her. She's covered in colorful food stains from her face to her knees—how did she get away with that?

# EARLY CHILDHOOD

Panorama of Shanghai Bund in 1930.
Source: http://www.fourthmarinesband.com/additional.htm, Author: US Signal Corps

My early childhood was spent in the exciting environment of Shanghai, the city referred to as the "Paris of the East," and oftentimes as "The Adventurer's Paradise," where the daily buzz was, at times, almost exquisitely unbearable.

The waterfront, known as "The Bund" (Hindustani translation), curved gently alongside the River and was eternally crowded with pedestrians, rickshaws, pedicabs, trams, cycles and cars. The whole area

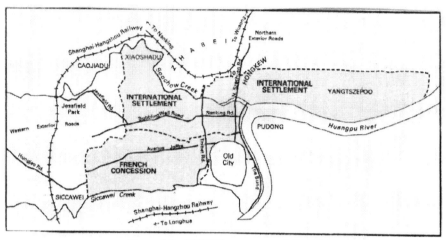

General Pre WWII layout map of Shanghai

throbbed with activity and deafening noises.

Ships' sirens and foghorns could be heard above the din, and the voices of the boat people carried over the water to join the street noises onshore. Vessels of all sizes, stationary, or moving in a small area, resembled a jigsaw puzzle with the pieces almost about to be locked into place.

Many boat dwellers lived their whole lives on the steamy, smelly Whangpu River, living under, by western standards, appalling conditions, with a savage mortality rate, all of which was accepted as pre-destiny. They had a quiet, resigned acceptance of death, believing "if one saved another's life one became responsible for the remainder of that life."

Fine restaurants, hotels, and large imposing buildings designed by prominent international architects stood facing the busy harbor. Tourists mingled with residents. People from all walks of life flocked to Shanghai to live, visit, work, or simply to escape and hide from some situation or authority in another country. For those of questionable moral character this was a safe haven.

Here and there, grunting, sweaty dockyard coolies, (the term derived from the Chinese word *ku-li*, meaning "bitter strength"), the menial, unskilled laborers, wearing baggy pants and bluish tunics, carried, pushed and pulled various loads. Filthy rags on their foreheads captured the sweat dripping from their brows. "Hey-ho, hey-ho" they chanted constantly, in unison, backs bending under heavy burdens.

Sounds and smells were strong, almost intoxicating, always inviting my imagination to race into unfamiliar territory.

Slender, elegant, well-groomed Chinese ladies wove their way unsteadily through teeming throngs of humanity, teetering on deliberately deformed, shrunken "lily" feet. How difficult it must have been for them to walk with dignity. I wondered why they didn't fall down. Oftentimes these were the ladies hidden in veiled palanquins, sedan chairs carried by coolies through the crowded, dirty streets of Shanghai. Sometimes they were wheeled in wheelbarrows, or carried to destinations on their servant's shoulders.

Painfully crippled, their tightly bound, mutilated stumps were clad in colorful, oftentimes exquisitely embroidered, tiny satin "lotus" shoes. Their abnormally arched, bound feet always remained concealed from men, who largely viewed the small steps, bodies waving like lilies, and the swaying "lotus" gait as desirable and the height of eroticism.

The incredibly cruel, torturous process of deforming and stunting the growth of feet was the ultimate manifestation of female subordination in China since the tenth century, and lasting around one thousand years. Beginning early in a girl's life—usually before the age of six—all her toes, but the first one, were broken and bent down and her feet were bound tightly with yards of silk or cloth strips, to prevent them from growing larger than about four inches. This was a continuous process, and although precautions were taken to prevent feet and toes from rotting, serious complications from infection and decay led to the death of some young girls.

Before, and for a while after the new Chinese republic banned foot binding in 1911, blood-chilling screams and wails were regularly heard emanating from behind the walls of Chinese homes where the foot-binding ceremony was taking place.

All but the poorest classes endured this crippling procedure. In many rural areas the practice continued for a number of years before finally coming to an end, even as late as 1949.


Where, I wondered, did the religious man with the shaved head, and those frighteningly fixated eyes, who beat on a little black *tok-box* all day, go when he left his dirty little street patch? A few holes cut out of the wooden box created a hollow sound of "tokking" that both frightened and intrigued me. And, although he seemed to be muttering in prayer, I could not discern any familiar sounds or words. I loved the thrilling sense of mystery and conjured up all kinds of mystical scenarios. Could he stand up straight after sitting so uncomfortably cross-legged for hours? Did he ever eat or sleep, or have a family somewhere? Could he simply disappear into the night sky? I had so many unanswered questions.

Liza Haviva Moses Yeheskel David Victoria Gracie Jack

JACOB ARZOONI FAMILY about 1920

# MY MATERNAL GRANDPARENTS

At the end of a tedious, lengthy sea voyage in 1918, the steamer carrying my maternal grandfather, Rabbi Yeheskel Jacob, finally entered the mouth of the Yangtze, situated about fifty-four miles from Shanghai. The river turned progressively yellow as it blended with the receding blue of the ocean. Against strong currents, the pilot navigated the vessel forty miles upstream to the Whampu, where it enters into the Yangtze, at Woosung.

Shanghai, Grandpa's future home for many years to come, was only fourteen miles away.

The passengers were amazed and excited by the unfamiliar alien sights, and the activity they encountered as the steamer made its way up the Whampu River. Foghorns blared, junks with bat-winged sails glided past, and mat-covered sampans hovered nearby. Some strange, unique, gaudily painted watercraft shared the river space. All managed somehow to avoid colliding. Chinese on vessels of varying sizes and shapes were cooking, hanging washing, carrying babies, and attending to their boats. Green fields and active farm life were visible on the riverbanks.

The steamer passed Pootung Peninsula on one side, and the long stretch of the Hongkew district, replete with dockyards and shipping piers, on the other. A grimy, dingy ambience pervaded the area that was jam-packed with warehouses, shipyards, cotton mills, lumberyards, billboards and countless storage sheds.

Finally they reached the harbor, where, anchored in a long line in the middle of the river, were the ever-present, huge, dominating warships of the colonial treaty powers— destroyers, troop carriers, battleships, and cruisers. Flags flying high, they represented Great Britain, America, Italy, France, and Japan.

A motley collection of smaller craft and tugboats floated and sailed around in close proximity to these giants.

Everyone gasped in amazement as the next sharp turn of the river brought the famous skyline of the International Settlement's Bund into view. Above a boulevard and grassy promenade, a conglomeration of imposing marble and granite buildings encompassing the architectural style of many cultures, formed a solid front. The palatial buildings included columns, sculptures, friezes, turrets, domes, and balustrades. On the top of the Customs House building, *Big Ching*, the clock from which the city set its time, was visible.

This was the introduction to Shanghai for Mummy's father. A sampan took him ashore to be welcomed by members of the Sephardic Community, for whom he was to multi-task and perform religious rituals. The city was, as yet, a mudflat with unpaved streets.

Grandpa was born in Northern Persia and ordained at *Beit Zilkha*, the prestigious rabbinical college in Baghdad. He was slightly built, with light skin, a small beard and sideburns curled behind his ears. A quiet, gentle, learned man, he was much loved and respected by the Jewish community and frequently consulted by those in need of his advice and wisdom. He always dressed in a suit, with a white shirt and bowtie. Of Sephardic origin, his attire contrasted dramatically with the rigid black dress code of the Ashkenazi orthodoxy, which had its roots in Europe and was modeled on the garb of sixteenth century European gentry.

As a student and teacher of *Kabala*, Jewish mysticism, he often spent most of the day sitting cross-legged in prayer and meditation, reminding me of the Chinese *tok-box* man. I searched for some meaningful connection, wondering whether their prayers would ultimately be heard by the same supreme, omnipotent God, who watched over everything He created on earth and in heaven. Were any of the multi-ethnic religious groups in China favored over others? The questions rolled around and around in my head—where did it all begin? I had no answers.

In 1919, one year after Yeheskel's arrival, his wife, Haviva, and their six children, Isaac, Victoria, Gracie, Jack, my mother Liza, and Moses, followed him. For the last time, after boarding the China-bound ship, she removed the black *abaya*, the robe-like dress worn by Islamic women, that she had worn since adolescence. Like a beautiful butterfly, she emerged from her cocoon—a well-dressed, well-groomed lady—anxious, but excited to finally reunite with her husband, and prepared to meet the challenges of her new life on a far-distant shore.

Mummy was then a lively young child. In 1921, David, their last child, was born in Shanghai. Sadly, during those difficult early days, they also suffered the untimely loss of an ailing infant daughter, Sarah Juliette.

Protective amulet worn by Jack, Liza's brother.

Unfortunately, I have been unable to discover the names of my maternal grandmother Haviva's family, who lived in Baghdad. My scant information comes from stories handed down and recounted by my mother, and other family members.

Granny was one of several siblings in a family that enjoyed a reasonably high standard of living. Like most Jews in their environment in the late 1880s, they had strong social networks and were religiously observant, offering prayers for every occasion. They were also quaintly superstitious, often wearing amulets to ward off the fearful "evil eye" and other dangers. The words *fachsit ein ha-rah*, crush the evil eye, were immediately intoned when a jealous gaze or praise was perceived as harmful.

My grandmother recounted a life-changing event about her father, who was a very strong man. Like Houdini, he prided himself on being able, after careful priming, to survive a blow to his stomach. The preparation, for which he was extensively trained, involved specialized tightening of his abdominal muscles.

One day, offering to demonstrate his strength to a group of people, he invited someone to punch his stomach with all the force he could muster. Before he had adequate time to prepare himself, the blow landed, smashing his organs, and bringing him to his knees. He collapsed on the ground. Tragically, massive internal bleeding caused his death.

The sudden devastating, unexpected loss of her husband speedily depleted my great-grandmother's resources, reducing the family to unimagined levels of poverty. Unable to cope with her mounting expenses, lowered living standard, and loss of social status, she negotiated an undisclosed transaction for Haviva's upkeep with a wealthy, orthodox Jewish family. At a very young age, my grandmother was sent from her parents' home to be companion and mother's helper to several young children of the new family.

Granny was a lovely-looking, obedient child. She said, "My mistress really liked me. It was so cold in winter. She used me to keep warm—making me sleep in her bed, at her feet. They treated me as one of the family," Granny recounted, "and I was able to visit my older married sister who lived in a big house nearby, with her husband's family—who came from Persia. My sister's husband was a drunkard, and abusive to her," she added sadly.

Haviva helped clean the house, and was taught to cook, sew, iron, and mend clothes. As she grew a little older, she was sent shopping for food and sundry items at the local markets. She learnt to bargain skillfully and to select the best fowls for ritualistic slaughter.

When Granny reached adolescence she, like all young girls, was compelled to don the black *abaya*, also known as *hijab*—the traditional over-garment worn by women in Baghdad. The large square of black fabric covered her whole body, except her feet and hands. A small veil covered her face, only exposing her beautiful, large brown eyes, genetically inherited eventually by several family descendants.

Some black *abayat* were embroidered, and other brightly colored ones had artwork on them, but as far as we know, Haviva only wore a simple, unadorned black abaya.

One day, her sister's mother-in-law saw the petite, attractive dark-haired young woman and proclaimed "That is the one I want for my son!" She was referring to Yeheskel, a rabbinical student—the only male not working in the family's successful goldsmith business.

Granny had, in fact, seen Yeheskel through a window while visiting her sister, and liked him enough to walk the extra distance to have chickens ritually slaughtered by the young schochet.

My own mother said, "My father saw my mother and fell in love." But Granny, always wearing the unrevealing *abaya* when she carried the chickens on their last live journey, said, "Your grandfather never saw me until our wedding ceremony."

We'll never find out what really happened, but the happy end result was two brothers marrying two sisters.

During Ottoman rule, Granny's mysteriously fair-haired, blue-eyed younger brother, Shuah, avoided conscription in the recruiting Turkish army by successfully pretending to be seriously mentally retarded. He drooled, slurred, and acted the role convincingly enough to be exempted without further ado.

One of Yeheskel's brothers was arrested and charged with practicing alchemy, the art of converting base metals into gold. Pronouncing him guilty, the judge sent him to prison for two years. Details of this event, and of his extensive experiments, are lost to us forever, but I have wondered about them ever since I heard the story many years ago.


A vision of my grandmother has been lodged in my memory since childhood. I remember well the embroidered Chinese slippers she always wore in the house, and how she usually wore her hair pulled tightly back in a bun. She was always very neatly attired.

Yeheskel and Haviva conversed in Judeo-Arabic, as did most Baghdadi and Middle Eastern Sephardic émigrés. They spoke neither English nor Chinese, making all general communication difficult, and depended heavily on translations by their children, who were speedily becoming conversant in English. With Amah's help, they were even acquiring a smattering of Chinese.

Many years later, I asked my mother how her parents communicated with their servants.

"Some broken Chinese—rubbish—and a little bit of broken English thrown in," she said.

"Granny could never talk to us—because she never learnt to speak good English," I said, ruefully.

"No she couldn't… she even learnt to read a little—*the cat sat on the mat*, and so forth—it wasn't good," Mummy said, matter-of-factly.

I had always wished I could converse with my grandmother. I wanted to know so much more about her life. I wondered how it might have impacted our family if my grandparents, like most immigrants, had applied themselves to becoming fluent in English. I'm certain my own life would have been greatly enriched through dialogue with them.

Many families had spent time in India and Burma before migrating to Shanghai, and for a long while continued to speak their original home languages. They were closely-knit and helped each other in their home and business lives, building ladders for others to climb after them.

Granny's days were extremely busy caring for so many young children, and she welcomed the Chinese amah's help in their new home. Once, I asked Mummy what it was like to be one of so many children. "Well," she replied, looking sadly into the distance, "I was very close to my mother— she loved us all. I realized that although she was a tired, overworked woman, she always found time to play with me in the afternoons. I used to help her in the kitchen, and we talked a lot. That's how we developed a really close relationship."

"That would probably apply in many large families," I reflected. "Now I know why you're such a fantastic cook." And truly, my mother can turn out a mouth-watering, gourmet feast in double-time, having very little to work with.

While passing on her culinary skills, Granny also managed to convey some "truisms" and wisdom to Mummy, who, whenever she repeated them, kept us in fits of laughter many times throughout the years. One particular saying in Arabic sounded something like this: *Imut il deek, ool einu bin nechala*, and translated roughly into: *The chicken (cock) is dead, but its eyes are still (fixed, looking) in the food bin!*

Every year before Yom Kippur, the most holy Jewish Day of Atonement, Grandpa circled a live fowl over our heads and repeated ritual prayers, which hopefully made the chicken do *Kappara*—the substitute for our sins. The chicken struggled and squawked in his firm grip on its legs and neck, while we stood, obediently still and wide-eyed, until he had finished the incantations. Then, producing a very sharp knife while still mumbling prayers, he would ritualistically cut the chicken's throat. The chicken continued to run, move, or twitch around while its last drops of lifeblood drained out.

This dramatic event was not wasted on us. It had a rather frightening theatrical appeal. I wondered whether the chicken's eyes were, indeed, "still looking in the food bin!" We awaited it each year, as did the Chinese servants who hovered unobtrusively around, trying not to show their amazement—or was it amusement?

Liza Jacob Arzooni, 1930s

# LIZA

The Jacob family lived on Dixwell Road, in a large, comfortable, multi-storied house, surrounded by their own private gardens and enough yard space for the children to play volleyball, badminton, and other games with their friends.

Mummy was the fifth of seven children. At junior school she was the top student every year. "My name is on the trophy, and if it's still around I suppose you'll see it," she said. To qualify her for the *Henry Leicester Scholarship* competition for complete school and university tuition, her teacher, Mrs. O'Toole, fudged her age from eleven to thirteen. Later, Mummy's brother, Isaac, put the incorrect age on her first passport—it led to our lifelong confusion and debates about her real age! Only her brother David, born in Shanghai, had a birth certificate. The others had their own methods of working out everyone's approximate birthdates, using Jewish holidays and seasonal changes as reference.

After completing Junior Cambridge at the Jewish School, Mummy attended Hanbury School for Girls, where she suffered from the effects of rife anti-Semitism. The Eurasians were the worst perpetrators. In Shanghai, no one escaped the levels of snobbishness and the caste system, starting from the top of the ladder and working it's way down, through the Chinese to their own menial laborers and poorest classes. The curriculum and exams adhered strictly to the English system, so as not to interrupt the studies of those returning "home" to England during their student years.

After three months she moved to the Public School for girls on Yu Yuen Road. It was a long daily bus ride from home, so her parents rented a house at one end of the same road as the school. My mother lived there until she married my father, who oddly enough, lived at the other end of the same road!

Although my father hadn't yet met my mother, she was in the same school class as his sister, Sally. Close friends, they took walks and studied together. Both were very clever students. "Sally excelled at mathematics—I wasn't very good at it, so she always helped me," Mummy said, "but I took all the prizes in other school subjects."

The two families mixed in different circles. "I never even saw them," Mummy told me. "I had sporting people—I played tennis and badminton, and went everywhere, competing with the Chinese and university people. I mixed with all sorts of people—Jews and Eurasians, people from the Cathedral and English schools. I also started diving when I was about fourteen."

"How did you start diving? Who taught you?" I asked.

"I always wanted to dive, and I trained myself."

"How did you manage to do all those somersaults, and everything?"

"Training—I went to the YMCA swimming pool on my own sometimes, when there was no one around, and tried to do the *gainer*. I just said, 'die, die, live, live,' and jumped *far* away from the board, turned back towards it, and dived in. But I landed on my back the first time, and was bruised all over!"

"And then what?" I asked, fascinated—trying hard to imagine it.

"Then, I went nearer and nearer, until I just *barely* brushed the edge of the board. Eventually, when I was twenty-six and already had three children, I won the Shanghai Diving Championship. It was international—against Chinese, Japanese, and everyone."

"Who was training all those people?"

"Other people—they came from different parts. I was watching them when they were teaching."

"Did you practice every day?"

"*Every* day! I used to go for two hours in the afternoon—from 12 to 2pm—and I dived, and after that I went to play volleyball, and we had wonderful fun. We also won the volleyball championship against the Chinese and Japanese, and everyone else."

"Who was on your team?"

"Six of us—some were Russians and some Eurasians."

I marveled at my mother's ability to have fun and her lifelong *joie de vivre*, no matter the adversities she faced.

Mummy told me her mother loved dancing and singing. "She had a beautiful voice and sang a lot. Although I didn't understand many of the lyrics, sung in the poetic language of her distant middle-eastern life, I relished hearing her clear flute-like tones, sung in a high register. She encouraged my own passion for dancing that started when I was two, by occasionally asking me to perform for visitors.

"I learnt many valuable lessons from my father," Mummy said. "Although he was very religious, he was never judgmental. He always raised his hand to demonstrate this, saying, 'Look at my fingers. Are they all the same? Just like your fingers, no two people are alike. If you tell someone not to do something wrong, and you know he's going to do it anyway, you double his sin. He is already aware that he is doing wrong—let him find out for himself.'

"Once my father was chastising two of my brothers. For some reason, he was very angry, and began hitting them. I was consumed with curiosity and stood too close. Suddenly, I was caught in the middle of it all and received some of the blows. I was an innocent bystander... my feelings were injured! I still wonder what my brothers did to receive such a hiding from my usually gentle father."

My mother's younger brother Moses was talented mechanically, but decidedly slower than all his siblings. She said, "He was really very mischievous—he loved practical jokes and was always playing tricks and pranks on everyone. Three months before my matriculation exams he pulled the chair out from under me as I sat. I fell down so hard I was seriously injured and unable to sit on a chair for a long time. I missed the exams and never got my certificate."

This painful episode must have been very difficult, and a great disappointment for my mother. Knowing her ability and how easily she coped with school and studying, I'm always saddened when I consider her lost opportunities...

Mummy enjoyed a particularly close relationship with her brother Jack, two years her senior. They shared many sporting and musical interests, and he accompanied her to outings and activities, guarding her when she was often the only girl in the group. She was highly respected and admired by the boys for her fearless, tomboyish traits, and treated as one of the gang.

When Jack was in his mid-teens Mummy encouraged him to take violin lessons and develop his musical talent. He practiced diligently, becoming a highly skilled professional violinist. I gather he was not very popular with some members of the family during his practicing sessions. Many years later he became a permanent member of the Israeli Philharmonic Orchestra. Uncle Jack was also a tenor, and sang operatic arias and popular songs of the era. Always questing for knowledge, he studied hypnosis, using himself, my mother, and his own father, as subjects. As far as I know, he didn't achieve any memorable results. "Sleep, sleep, you're falling sleep," he would say to his father.

"All right—I'm asleep already. I'm dreaming," was my grandfather's amused response.

Mummy was also extremely artistically talented. She longed for piano lessons, but no one offered to pay for them. Her older sister Gracie bought a piano and kept it locked, so my mother never had a chance to play it. Auntie Gracie never played it either. My mother said, "I cried and cried—it was so mean!" She pursued her love of dancing instead, performing on stage, putting on shows, and teaching various dance genres. She became a successful oil-painting artist after turning fifty, and continued teaching yoga into her nineties. Nothing daunted her.

In summer, my mother took cruises with her brother and sisters to close-by, popular destinations. They went to Dairen, Tsingtao and other islands for summer holidays and took cheap accommodation, sometimes sleeping overnight on the deck with many other travelers. "We took cushions and whatever we needed to make ourselves comfortable," she said. "The decks were crowded, we were young, and it was fun. It was very hot, so we didn't need any blankets."

On Sundays, as a rule, Mummy and Jack took a two-hour ferry ride to a small-scale pleasure resort area—possibly called Henley—on the Pootung side of the river. "We used to go to swim, and we spent the whole day there," she said. "We also used to climb onto bridges, which were derelict, really—broken here and there—and we used to jump. Every few hundred yards a wooden pier jutted way out, and," she continued, "we used to go to the cranes. We climbed up and balanced precariously. As usual, I said, 'die, die, live, live,' and we dived into the filthy, dirty water! By the time we came up... We were lucky. It was terrible, really—because there were dangerous spikes in the river!"

"You used to take a lot of chances," I said, finding it hard to imagine how my mother could be so daring. She always uttered the same mantra before undertaking some daredevil action.

"Yes—that's so. I loved that, I think—but that was when I was young… It was also extremely hazardous where we jumped, because it was perilously close to the dividing line between the river and the ocean. It was clearly visible—the dirty yellow and the blue water, both going in different directions. We could easily have been swept away!" My mother's evocative recall, always related in a breathless fashion, caused my own heart to skip a beat or two.

Great-grandmother Matana Nissim early 20th Century

Upper photo: Great-grandmother Matana Nissim early 20th century.

Lower photo: Matana Isaacs and Matook Nissim wedding photo, 1890.

# GREAT-GRANDMOTHER MATANA

My paternal great-grandmother, Matana, was born in 1871, on a junk, in Chingkiang, where the Grand Canal intersects the Yangtze River. She was referred to as a "change-of-life" baby.

Soon after her birth, the family moved to Shanghai, where she attended the only foreign school for girls, run by French nuns, and became fluent in French.

At nineteen, she married Matook Nissim who was born in Allahabad, British India, now known as Pakistan. He was a very short, good-looking man, who, because of his blue eyes, freckles, and sand-colored hair, was often taken for an Irishman.

My great-grandfather completed his education in English, and claimed he continued on to first-year medical school in London. He brought his medical textbooks with him to China and referred to them constantly, diagnosing all ailments.

Family legend claims he spent time in Siberia before arriving in China via the overland silk route, accompanied by a group of Cossacks. Occasionally they went hunting together in the backcountry. He spoke fluent Russian and danced the *Trepak*, a Russian dance, while juggling chairs.

After my grandmother, Essie, was born, Matana took ill with childbed fever (puerperal fever) and was renamed Rahma, in a customary effort to "change one's luck for the better."

When my great-grandfather died in 1924, Rahma moved into her married son's large opulent home, on Quinsan Road.

They entertained frequently and lavishly. Some parties ran for several days and nights on end. Guests, comprising of relations and close friends, played cards and mahjong, or socialized, while an endless stream of trays, loaded with delicious food, were brought from the kitchen and offered to them. Whisky, wine, and fresh fruit juices flowed generously and freely into crystal glasses. The house was a hive of activity and chatter, and a generally high-spirited atmosphere prevailed. People arrived and left, some surrendering their places at the card tables to sleep, or have a rest in one of the rooms in the house, before resuming play.

Great-grandmother chewed paan, the Betel-leaf—a known carcinogen linked to high levels of oral cancer. A type of digestive, the habit was age-old and deeply rooted in India, where it was popular as a breath freshener and palate cleanser. It was frequently offered to visitors and guests, as a sign of hospitality, to be eaten at social and cultural events.

In most Indian provinces, Betel-leaf eating has great significance in wedding rituals. The folded leaves, filled with various ingredients, including cardamom and areca nuts, with its narcotic value, are distributed at wedding parties. Paan could be mixed with sugar, spices and fresh or candied fruit, and wrapped in a triangular leafy package, held together with a toothpick. Sometimes it was mixed with tobacco—heightening its cancer-causing risks.

Ornate, perforated Betel boxes, some created in the shapes of flowers, fruit and colorful birds, were once an integral part of households, and commonly a part of the gifts from their respective fathers-in-law to the bride and bridegroom. The perforations in the beautiful boxes—that are today Indian artefacts—prolonged the freshness of the leaves.

Makeshift Paan shops, located at most street corners, are run by *paan wallahs*, as the sellers are called, and are a part of Indian culture. After meals, people make their way to the tiny shops, where they share entertaining stories and information, and purchase paan. In this way, a centuries-old culture, that infiltrated and proliferated so much of Asia, is being kept alive.

In great-grandmother's house, many decorative, colorful spittoons were placed in convenient places for use by paan-chewing guests. They took careful aim, because chewed betel-leaf, with combinations, produced a red-colored juice that left unsightly stains. I remember watching my tiny great-grandmother's mouth constantly moving, only stopping briefly when she spat into a nearby, multicolored receptacle.

When I was nine, in 1947, great-grandmother's years of paan-addiction caused the cancer in her cheek that finally claimed her life.

"Grandmother's gone," Daddy announced tearfully, when he returned from the big house, after spending many hours with other family members, gathered together to pray and bid "farewell" to their beloved Rahma.

The whole family, and the Sephardi Jewish community, paid their respects at the huge funeral, and visited the house in droves to express condolences at the demise of one of the pillars of our community. All were truly saddened by the loss. She was a sweet, generous, wonderful woman, who continued to live vividly in my own memory, and to appear many times in my dreams.

No more marathon parties ever took place in that house. Soon we would all leave Shanghai, scattering to the four corners of earth, many never to see each other again.

Grandmother Essie Benjamin (nee Nissim)

Top L. Essie Benjamin. Yu Yuen Road house.
Top R David and Essie Benjamin.

Bottom L. David and Essie Benjamin
Wedding Photo. May 1909.

Upper bottom R. Benjamin house in Yu Yuen
Road.

Lower Bottom R. Benjamin Daughters. L to
R—Sally, Eva, Leah, Eileen.

# THE BENJAMINS

My Paternal grandmother, Essie, was a tall, slender, aristocratic, and rather haughty looking woman. We called her Un-noo, which is "Grandma" in Hindustani. She had a lofty, regal carriage and dominated all who surrounded her.

When seventeen-years-old and barely past her own childhood, she married David Hai Benjamin, whose family had come from Bombay. Soon my father, Benjy, the first of their six children, was born. He was her favorite child, on whom she doted. She indulged him shamelessly and he basked in her affection, accepting all the perks that went with being the eldest male child in a Sephardic home. She excused his temper tantrums and bad moods, and he dominated his brother Syddie and sisters Leah, Sally, Eva and Eileen.

My grandfather, David, was a quiet-spoken, successful businessman known as the *Chemor King*, because he held the largest number of shares in two rubber plantations in Chemor, British Malaya—now known as Malaysia. He was also an import and export dealer and leased large warehouses, called *godowns* in Asia, where merchants could store incoming and outgoing goods in the wharves along the bustling Whampu River's edge.

The Benjamins lived on Yu Yuen Road, in an imposing twenty-four roomed double-storey mansion, complete with tennis court, swimming pool, and beautifully tended gardens. Inside, lush hand-woven Chinese and Persian carpets covered floors, and heavy brocade and velvet curtains adorned the windows. Beautifully carved blackwood furniture, silver ornaments, and often-used silver dinnerware needed regular attention and polishing. Twelve servants that included two each of Japanese amahs, Chinese house "boys," cooks, menial laborers, and gardeners, kept the house in good order.

Two Indian Sikh watchmen in brightly colored turbans guarded the large, iron front gate. They slept in their own quarters, a little stone hut, where they cooked and ate delicious-smelling Indian food. The mouthwatering aroma sometimes wafted across the large front gardens.

Often, after attending Sabbath services at the Sephardic Ohel Rachael Synagogue, many guests were invited to share a sumptuous feast in the beautiful home and surrounding gardens. White-jacketed servants, bearing large platters of aromatic food and delicacies, wove their way efficiently between the visitors. Soiled monogrammed silverware and crockery was speedily replaced with a seemingly endless supply of clean dinnerware.

Many of the fashionably attired guests were related, and felt comfortable with each other. They mingled freely, discussing topics of the day and gossiping about the latest scandals. Children played games and chased each other around in the gardens. The family-oriented community indulged their happy laughter and shouts.

For the most part, foreigners in Shanghai lived apart from the Chinese, in enclaves named the "International Settlement," where we lived with the predominantly British and American population, and the "French Concession," which mainly housed French and European nationals. It was known for its attractive European and art deco style architecture and wide tree-lined streets.

Afternoon "tea dances" at hotels, restaurants, clubs, and other places, were a popular pastime. At most venues, pieces of paper called "chits" were frequently signed as promissory notes for later payment of all services.

No foreigners lived in the Chinese city, an area once girded since the sixteenth century by a brick wall.

Essie was extremely socially driven and David bowed to her domination, allowing her every wish to be his command. The word "no" was not part of his vocabulary, so she was able to spend lavishly on her home and personal attire. Every year she bought a new fur coat and, drawing herself up to full height had herself professionally photographed while wearing it, preening haughtily in front of the family home.

Daddy was soon the tallest member of the family. Mummy always described him as "tall, dark and handsome." Both brothers grew to be attractive, immaculately well- groomed men, who wore hand-tailored suits, fedoras, and spats, to races and social events. They had visible, starched white handkerchiefs in their pockets, carried gloves, and wore gold fob watches.

Daddy's sisters were fine-looking women, who adhered to the latest fashion dictates. Shanghai's huge department stores, Wing On, Sincere, Sun-Sun and the Sun Company, on Nanking Road, were stocked with a bewildering array of the latest haute couture from around the world. Tailors running small designer businesses could make any fashionable item of clothing within hours, and beautiful hand-made shoes took the same amount of time. Silk dresses and suits were popular, and ladies looked glamorous in hats, veils, matching gloves and elegant shoes.

Grandfather owned six racehorses that occasionally won big prizes at the Shanghai racecourse. "They were so lucky," Mummy told me, "Especially when he won what was called a *clodhopper*, because every time it rained that horse came first! You got real money!" Mummy said. "But altogether, the Benjamins were well-known for their luck in gambling—anything like that. They always returned from the racecourse with their bags *full* of money! Always, always, always! That's it! My mother-in-law went with an empty bag and sometimes she couldn't close it—because it was bulging with her winnings!"

"Wow!" I said. "And—did they all, *always*, dress up and go?"

"Yes. We *had* to dress up—hats, gloves, high heels, and lovely clothes—beautiful things..."

"And afterwards, did they have a party at the racecourse?"

"No—people went to have a drink and meet friends in the members clubhouse. I still have my membership badge."

"Obviously, a lot of Jewish people owned racehorses."

"Yes—the highest one was Sir Victor Sassoon," Mummy said. "He had wonderful horses. Once, when I was twelve, I rode one..."

"You could ride?" I was surprised. Was this another of my mother's talents?

"Oh yes—I tried it, that's all... a huge horse—I hated it! I could hardly walk for a week!"

"You're like me—I can't even sit on a horse," I said. "I tried it once and also hated it!" I remembered my abject fear, as a child, of being thrown off the animal's neck, where I had been seated in front of two other young children. The horse kept ducking, and I kept screaming! It was my nightmare!

Everyone dressed in finery to attend, be seen, and socialize freely at the races. A lot of businesses closed on racing days so people could attend what was considered a regular and exciting social event, and where many business deals were concluded with a handshake. The British attributed great importance to two things in particular—the king and the races!

Stylish, affluent Chinese men accompanied by beautiful, exotic-looking women, were regular visitors to the races, adding color to the event. They enjoyed gambling, a favorite pastime in China.

Hundreds of Chinese crowded outside the fence to watch, and Indian Sikhs in colorful turbans sat in circles on grassy areas around the racecourse, chatting loudly with each other. Women were excluded from these groups.

"Did you go to the races a lot—before the war?" I asked my father.

"Yes," he said. "Once, my great friend, Charlie Liang, came over and said, 'Benjy, you're a member, eh—of the race club? Buy a lotto ticket, and I'll sell to people. And why don't we keep your name and my name on the back?'

"And every November and March the Championship races came. Then—I was out learning how to drive a car, and I didn't know until I got home..." Daddy was excited, "I called out, 'Mama! Come down quickly!' As soon as Charlie returned to our house I asked him, 'What would you like—first, second, or third prize?' He said, 'First, of course!' We won third prize—$25,000! Half-half with him."

I was caught up in Daddy's excitement, and unable to imagine its probable staggering present-day equivalent. "Wonderful! Did you also win with your father's horses?"

"Yes—and I lost it gambling!"

"Was that big money?" I was surprised by his admission—even though I was aware how much enjoyment the family derived from gambling. It was a popular pastime for many with, or without, means.

"Oh yes—big!"

"What happened to the horses?"

"They ate them! How do I know?" Daddy replied, sarcastically, obviously uneasy with this subject.

"Did you lose the horses *before* the war?"

"Yes sure—before the war. Around 1931."

"They just disappeared—that was it? You have no idea? Maybe your mother sold them?" I was beginning to realize it was during the period of my grandfather's great financial losses.

"I don't know!" He responded tersely.

My father appeared distressed and was obviously losing patience.

"Maybe my father sold them," he said, with a sharp finality that ended my probing.


The family regularly travelled by ship to India, Burma, Manila, Japan, and other Far Eastern destinations. They took their cook, amah, and "boy" with them, and occupied an entire suite. Such was their opulent lifestyle—no expense was spared.

In 1925 Essie and all six children travelled on a P&O liner to India—via Hong Kong, Singapore, Columbo, Penang and Karachi. Years later Auntie Eileen told me, "My straw hat blew out the window and sailed onto the ocean, where I watched it float out of sight. I was only seven or eight years old, and I cried my head off!"

My grandfather joined them three months later. First they all stayed with relatives, and then they moved to an apartment opposite a jail, where convicts in white robes and chained ankles could be seen moving around and working. Eileen said, "At night we heard lions roaring loudly at a nearby zoo. It was frightening!"

# MUMMY MEETS DADDY

Benjy, 1930's.

"So Mummy, you went to a wedding where you met Daddy?"

"Yes—my eldest sister Victoria's wedding."

"Was that a big wedding?" I asked.

"Yes—in Shanghai, every Jewish wedding had to be a big wedding, because we invited the whole community."

"Was there a band playing?"

"Yes," Mummy said, "*always* there was a live band."

Liza, 1930's.

"And what was Daddy doing? Sitting in on it?"

"Daddy went in, took the piano over and was playing… he always did that. They all knew him— the Chinese people, the other people, wherever he went. Even when we went on a boat he used to do that!" Mummy was obviously enjoying her memory of that moment.

"Ok, so you went over to listen and you were fascinated by him?"

"No—I wasn't fascinated by him at all. I just asked him to play *Roses of Picardy*, because I was dancing. I was a young girl and I was dancing with the others. He was a big fellow, who appeared to me like an elderly man—nothing to do with me."

"Oh! Really?" I said. "Like an elderly man… hmm!"

"He was BIG and heavy!" She surprised me with her adamant description.

"Was he? Really?" It was difficult to visualize my good-looking father through her eyes.

"Yes. You can see pictures of him… he had a big stomach!"

"And then, you said Sally invited you to tea… do you think that was initiated by her mother—or by herself?"

"By her mother. That's what they told me afterwards."


"Daddy," I asked, curious to hear his version of their meeting, "Did you know Mummy when she was younger?"

"She was seven years younger than me, and then her sister got married, and they invited our family. So, I heard music, and I always went first to the band—to see what's going on. Then *she* came—and she's so small, she put her head, and her whole body over the table—looking at me. She said, 'You'll play the piano for us now?' I said, 'All right.' She was hanging on. Then…" My father demonstrated—singing the popular tune he played while my mother was draped over the piano!

"You played that?" I asked.

"Yes—and they all started clapping. She was so happy! So," Daddy continued, "when I went home, Sally started following my mother around, saying, 'She looked so pretty, her face, her costume…' And my mother said, 'All right! If you like her so much—just call her.' So, she came to the house and that was the day…"


"Oh. So they invited you to tea, Mummy, and *he* opened the door?"

"And stood there…"

"Gazing at you…"

"Yes."

"And did you meet the whole family that day—was everybody there?"

"Yes. Everyone. And he wouldn't let me go home until it was quite late at night."

"So the chauffeur took you home that night?"

"That's right. We lived near them, on Yu Yuen Road. They were the first house and we were the last. Then they moved to a very big house—before I got married."

"Oh. After that, did he call you and take you out?"

"Not yet—no. One or two months. They were always inviting me, and coming over to our house—and we had games and fun." Mummy, sounding like a young girl, was really enjoying this account! "Every time I went there, he tried his best to get friendlier with me. The girls used to resent his being there, because he was older than them."

"And then what happened? He invited you out, and then?" I, too, was enjoying her youthful recollections.

"Then I said, 'I—I—you take my sister…' I told him to take Gracie, because she was older, and I wasn't thinking of anything—going out with him. He appeared to be so much older, somehow. I said, 'Gracie can come too.' He told me the table was not for three people, only for two!"

I found this really amusing. "Hmm! Was he good-looking—do you think?"

"*Very* good-looking! Both boys were very, very handsome."

"During all that time he was trying and everything, did you ever see his mother?"

"All the time! She was very, very fond of me."

"And was she nice to you?"

"Yes. She used to do the table—the Ouija board—and she used to make the table move. She loved talking to me about spiritual subjects, because I was into that a lot."

"And did the table really move?"

"They always upped the table…"

"She—oh! I see. So you think she was rigging it?" I almost wished I had been there to see it happening. "So she was very sensationalist, in other words?"

"Yes," Mummy said, with relish, and much giggling.

"And, did she have a lot of friends?"

"Yes—people always came to the house. The table was laden…"

"Is that why they came—because of the food, or because they liked her?"

"She was very entertaining with friends. There were one or two people who were regulars, as a matter of fact, who just came to eat, really. Because they didn't have anything."

I knew my grandmother was charitable and extremely hospitable. She welcomed people into their home. "And did they speak English all the time?"

"Yes—all the time. They also had a great sense of humor and laughed a lot. My mother-in-law had a habit—when smiling or laughing—of turning her hand up, raising her thumb, and gazing at the nail." My mother demonstrated the strange action.

"Why did she do that?"

"I don't know—no one could ever explain the origin or meaning. It remained a secret forever."

"How long did you go with Daddy before he asked you to marry him?"

"I didn't go with him… he invited me out! In the end, at last, I said, 'All right.' And then, when we went out, he asked me to marry me."

I was stunned! "Before he had even been taking you out everywhere?"

"Yes—because he was seeing me in the house, and all. We were always in groups when we were young. We went to the cinema in groups, and to Wing On's and Sincere's to buy all sorts of Chinese dried fruit, and things like that. And we all went in two cars sometimes, and that's how it was. Wherever we went, he came."

"Always in groups?" I was really surprised. "He had a car for himself— with a chauffeur?"

"Yes. He had his own car. The chauffeur would drive the car, and he drove it too. Sometimes, while waiting at the bus stop when I was younger, I used to see him ride past in a horse-drawn carriage."

"So, he asked you to marry him in the Rosemarie restaurant?"

"Yes—and I was *so* overcome, I was so shy that I suddenly found myself under the table. I really slipped right down! I couldn't answer—I was *so* shy!"

It's hard to imagine my mother being shy. I've really always seen her as feisty and unafraid of challenges! "Did you think he was going to ask you to marry him?"

"No! I thought he was just asking me to go out—because I used to go out with a lot of people—boys and girls together, always. Then somehow, after a while, the others dwindled down. I was more in their group for a while, you see."

"Did he go and ask your father if you could marry him?"

"Oh yes! *After* he asked me."

"Were they happy?"

"No—my father didn't want me to get married. He said my older sister was not married yet—she was six years older. There was Jack in between, don't forget."

This was an old-fashioned custom. "So what did he want—that Gracie should marry first, and *then* you'd marry? Is that why?"

"Partly. He always said, 'Not for you maybe—he's too old for you.'"

"He said that?"

"Yes."

"So what was the age difference between Daddy and his brother Syddie? Was he older?"

"Syddie was six months older than me."

"So he was more your age—a young boy." Although I never saw much of my uncle because of the war and his subsequent emigration, in 1948, I have a vivid recollection of his slim, youthful appearance. He was very fond of me, and treated me gently, like a pet. I always sat on his knee. "Whom do you love?" he would ask me, whilst looking at my mother.

"And we were more inclined towards sports and all. I was very friendly with him—in a very nice way. He played tennis—I loved tennis. Daddy was not crazy about sports at all. He didn't like swimming. Syddie was a good swimmer."

"So, now you were engaged—how long did your engagement last, and did you have a nice ring?"

"Yes, a very nice one—almost two carats. The ring was later on stolen by one of the servants who looked after my little boy, who was a year old."

"How long did you know Daddy before he asked you to marry him. Was it a year? Six months? He only came into your crowd after…"

"Into my life—the Sunday after my sister's wedding. Only about two or three months. I got engaged in October, just before my birthday."

"About two or three months in the crowd—that's all?"

"Yes. But I saw a lot of him, because the girls kept on calling me. They used to come and take me, bring me. They had to have me with them every day! We had fun together, actually. And they were trying to reject him out of sight. They said, 'Go away Benjy—leave us alone! Stop pestering us!'"

Mummy was laughing heartily, vividly recalling these scenes from her youth. "Eventually," she continued, "they gave up, and reluctantly allowed him to join in our games. He became happier and less controlled, lost weight from all the added activity, and never regained the "plump" appearance of his childhood—which made his mother very happy! Before he met me he was a rather prim and proper young man."

Actually, the photos I have of my father as a young man clearly portrayed that image.

"You said that at some point you didn't want to get married. You were very worried because Daddy had a bad temper. We all knew that."

"I saw him lose his temper with one of the Chinese servants, so I broke off the engagement. I didn't want to… and he kept on coming and crawling, and coming and crawling, until almost two months passed."

"Did he hit the servant?"

"Not at all!"

"Just screamed and shouted at her?" I asked.

"And a bad temper—I didn't like the temper. His mother came, his grandmother came, his uncles came—everybody came to talk to me, you know—they didn't want me to give him back his ring!"

"So you gave it back, and then you finally agreed to it again?"

"Yes. He tried to rush the wedding, and I said, 'I want to wait two years, because I don't want to get married so quickly.' I had just turned eighteen when I got married! It's not right, and I was so inexperienced. I was scared of marriage, actually."

"Then you had a very big wedding—more than six hundred people. Where did you live when you got married—in the house with your in-laws?"

"Yes. After the wedding we lived in *their* house."

Benjy and Liza's Wedding Shanghai 1935

Benjy and Liza's Wedding Cake -- Shanghai Astor House Hotel 1935

# BENJY AND LIZA'S WEDDING

My parents married in the late afternoon hours of February 17, 1935. Rabbi Hirsch consecrated their vows at Ohel Rachel Synagogue, on Seymour Road. The imposing structure, built in March 1920 by Sir Jacob Elias Sassoon—the prominent, wealthy Sephardic Baghdadi Jew—was endowed in memory of his wife, Lady Rachel.

Wide balconies overlooked the sanctuary, and marble pillars flanked the walk-in ark that once held thirty Torah scrolls. In 1923 my father celebrated his Bar Mitzvah in the beautiful new synagogue that could accommodate up to seven hundred people. At the time Shanghai's Sephardic Jews numbered between five and seven hundred.

A few months prior to the synagogue's completion Sir Jacob died, and the community decided to dedicate it to both him *and* his wife.

My mother was a beautiful bride, recalled by a man who remembered her seventy years after her wedding, as "an extremely pretty young woman." It was no secret she was eyed as a desirable "catch." She often told me she had declined thirty-two marriage proposals—including Chinese men—before accepting my father's. One ardent suitor threatened to throw himself off Shanghai's tallest building if she refused him! "Then do it!" she responded, but he never did. She was extremely chaste, and had never been kissed by any man other than my father, who was equally chaste and naïve!

My father, because of his regal carriage and dark good looks, was also regarded as a "catch," and referred to by many Jews and Chinese as a "prince." Like his mother, he was rather proud and snobbish, and not above averting his eyes at times, or not turning to look at people he didn't wish to acknowledge.

On their wedding day, my petite mother's perfectly proportioned person radiated charm and beauty. Her older sisters, Gracie and Victoria, helped my mother get dressed. Victoria was her maid-of-honor. Her long, clinging, lace-trimmed, creamy-white satin gown had sleeves of elbow-length satin, extending to the wrists with flaring hand-woven lace. It was embroidered with pearls. The heavy satin train was three yards long, and lifted by two young cousins. She wore very high heels. Then, she put a blue garter around her thigh, honoring the superstitious instruction to wear *Something Old, Something New, Something Borrowed, Something Blue*. She had designed her own gorgeous dress, and skillful Chinese tailors painstakingly hand-sewed it within one week, during which time they came to my grandparents' house for just three fittings. The dress was extremely expensive, costing over $200. At the time it was a large sum.

My father, his brother Syddie, and my mother's brothers looked splendid in dress suits and top hats. All my aunts were bridesmaids. The family stood on the steps of my paternal grandmother's mansion and posed for group wedding photos.

Both sets of grandparents gave my mother a substantial allowance for her trousseau. She shopped at Shanghai's gigantic department stores on Nanking Road, spending lavishly, and selecting carefully from their bewildering array of beautiful clothes and delicate handmade lingerie.

Although my father's family was struggling financially through the hard years following the depression in 1929, my grandmother borrowed huge sums of money to pay for her favorite son's wedding, insisting it had to be a grandiose affair in keeping with the Benjamin name. She ably took complete charge of every detail. At that time only my father's sister, Leah, was already married.

More than six hundred guests attended the reception, a tea dance, held in two huge ballrooms at the fashionable Astor House Hotel, located on the north side of Garden Bridge, on Huangpu Road. Many famous visitors had stayed there over the years—President Ulysses S. Grant, Albert Einstein, ragtime composer Scott Joplin, philosopher Bertrand Russell, and Charlie Chaplin. The prestigious building was the first to introduce electric lighting in China.

As was customary, the entire Sephardic Jewish community was invited. Friends from different ethnic and religious denominations were included. A significant number of Chinese business associates and acquaintances were invited, and mingled freely with other guests. The men wore beautifully hand-tailored wool suits, or long, exquisitely embroidered brocade and silk gowns. The women were elegantly adorned in elaborate, indescribably beautiful, Chinese handcrafted, vivid silks and satins. Jews and Chinese enjoyed a comfortable level of shared mutual respect for each other's religious beliefs and similar values.

The resplendent five-tiered wedding cake was the center of attraction on the largest of several tables that held an abundance of cakes, sandwiches, and tea-party delicacies. Elegant crystal wine decanters, expensive whisky and other liquor, fresh fruit juice, and additional platters of delicious food, continued to pour from the kitchen as guests arrived. A profusion of artistically arranged flowers permeated the ambience with perfume. No expense was spared for the occasion.

Guests danced to the music of different big bands in the two crowded ballrooms—separated by three steps—only stopping to hear speeches, and raise their glasses in a toast to the bride and groom. They twirled around, the ladies' long, colored eveningwear creating a lovely rainbow. Diamonds and precious stones, set in elaborately crafted gold jewelry, glittered on both men and women. Shanghai's elitist society was living up to its name—loving the high-life of the 1930s.

Following the reception, the entire extended family, and a large number of special guests, proceeded to my father's house. As the evening wore on, a sumptuous, multi-course kosher dinner, prepared by leading Chinese caterers, was served. Quiet-footed Chinese waiters, in starched white jackets and long black pants, padded unobtrusively between tables, replacing dishes and cutlery. Finger bowls, filled with water and a slice of lemon, were used between courses by guests happily awaiting the next surprise treats offered. The party continued into the early morning hours, with unlimited supplies of food and liquor freely available.

For seven days thereafter, in accordance with a largely observed custom, family and friends were invited to lavish dinners, and the *Sheva Brachot*—the Seven Blessings—were recited. "My parents were always there," my mother said. "I was just a bride, and did nothing. The house was full of people at all times of day, arriving and leaving in a steady stream."

My parents never went on honeymoon. I asked my mother how she felt at the time. "I was so young," she replied. "I regarded the whole thing as a romantic affair. Anyway, the house was so big... there were many places we could escape to for some private moments together."

My mother said, "Wonderful, expensive wedding gifts were piled high on tables at Astor House and at home, but we received very few of them. "A lot of it," she recounted wistfully, "was valuable silverware and cut glass, given by wealthy Jewish and Chinese guests."

My grandmother commissioned most of it to recoup and repay the money she borrowed to finance the unforgettable, widely reported "Shanghai wedding of the year."

# KIDNAPPED!

After the wedding, as was widely accepted practice at the time, my parents went to live with my grandparents and the rest of the family, on Yu Yuen Road.

My mother was very fond of her father-in-law. "He was such a nice man," she said, "so friendly and loving—and he used to look at me so sadly… with an apologetic expression in his eyes, and face. I wondered why… And he always used to tell me about his adventures when he went on safari."

"Where did he go on safari?" I asked.

"India."

"India?" This made sense to me, since my grandfather was born in Bombay and was very comfortable spending time in his childhood country.

"Yes—he was a great sportsman that way—when he was younger. He was really a nice, kind, well-travelled man."

"Was he good to his wife? Were they happy?" I wanted to know. "I think he loved her a lot…"

"He loved her—she was very good-looking," Mummy said.

"Did she dominate him?" How I wished I could transport myself back to that era and spend time with my ancestors, who, more and more, were finding a place in my heart. I wanted to climb through the windows on the photograph and enter the big house they shared in 1935.

"She was a dominant woman, altogether," Mummy said, " but she was charming, when she wanted to be. Good-looking and tall—she looked after her figure. She had a nice face…"

"But she was a snob!" I had heard this description of my grandmother so many times.

"Yes—she was snob, but she was also very kind to poor people—she was always taking people who were ill to hospital. There you are—two sides to the coin…"

"Were her children scared of her?" I asked.

"She dominated everybody," Mummy said, matter-of-factly. "If *she* got angry with somebody, everybody else must be angry too."


During the Great Depression, Grandfather had great difficulty maintaining his wealth and family's living standards. He was able to recover twice, but the third time, one loss led to another, and he sank lower and lower into a black well of depression. Finally bankrupted in 1935, and no longer able to bear his pain, he took his own life. He relieved his wife and children of the burden of police enquiry by committing this final act in a locked bathroom at the racecourse—the very place where he had spent so many pleasurable hours of his life.

"And who discovered him?" I was shocked to hear these details.

"The people there. They saw the blood… there were so many people doing it at that time—all over the world. Not only in Shanghai. And then, everything turned chaotic—from a brilliant wedding to mourning… and it changed *everything* for us."

"He waited two years, after buying insurance, to do it," I said, having heard this from another relative, "so his wife would get the money."

"That's right—and she got it. But she had to wait," Mummy said sadly. "I was really so sorry when he died. It broke everything up. Everything went topsy-turvy! Everybody went mad—it was horrible, horrible, horrible!"

"And the newspapers were full of it—for ages?"

"Oh yes! Like the wedding—the wedding filled the newspapers in the beginning, then the mourning filled the newspapers afterwards. He was a well-known businessman. The Chinese papers were also full of it. And the people who came to mourn for him were from every strata of the community. Jewish people, Chinese people, others and others… He was well loved—that's how it was…"

The shocked family was overcome with grief. Grandmother was traumatized to the point of a breakdown. "No! No!" she screamed when told the terrible news. She, and all her children, cried incessantly, unable to accept what was beyond their comprehension.

"Why, why?" My father, immobilized by his pain, was unable to get up from the floor, where he sat thrashing about and howling.

My parents, so recently married, struggled to cope with a catastrophe of such magnitude, and the inevitable subsequent consequences. In one day, their entire world was turned inside out. Benjy was only twenty-four years old. As the first-born child, and older son, the heavy weight of responsibility descended on his young shoulders.

Relatives and friends gathered around in support of the devastated family. Struggling with drastically reduced material standards, Essie eventually gave up the beautiful home where she lived for so many years, and where all her children were born and raised. Feeling embarrassed and ashamed to have reached this degrading impasse, she gratefully accepted a kind relative's offer to move the whole family into two rooms of his house.

After grandfather's tragic demise, Essie underwent a dramatic personality change. Her normally kind disposition towards my mother turned into blind, unreasonable jealousy over her son's love for his new bride, a lovely young woman with a happy, peace-loving disposition. Relentlessly, she imposed a tyrannical rule over her, seeking any reason to complain about the slip of a girl, then just eighteen years old.

My brother, David, was born in November 1935. As was customary in Sephardic tradition, he was named after our grandfather, David Benjamin.

My grandmother controlled every aspect of the baby's life. "Don't touch him!" she would command, taking David, her first newly born grandchild away from Liza. "He's mine. My child!"

Liza's doubled efforts to please her mother-in-law met with little success. One day, Essie, in a fit of temper, screamed, "What is a wife but an old shoe? You can throw her down the stairs."

Liza left Benjy and returned with her baby to her parents' home. Every month she took him to the clinic to be weighed, and have his general progress assessed. One day her brother, Moses, acting as her bodyguard, accompanied her. As they walked home down Tifen Road, Liza recognized Benjy's black car parked nearby. She saw him and his Chinese chauffeur and realized with a rush of panic that they were lying in wait for her. Benjy speedily approached them, and a fierce street fight erupted between Daddy and my uncle. The chauffeur grabbed the baby from the stroller.

"Come home with me. Please Liza, please come home," my father, now weeping, begged my stunned, inconsolable mother.

"No, no! I can't ever go back to that house. Benjy—please don't do this! I beg you, give me back my baby." My mother's pleas were unsuccessful. In disbelief, she watched the car drive away with David, her tiny baby.

A small crowd of Chinese passersby had gathered to witness this strange event between the "foreign devils." Liza, panic stricken and sobbing with grief, returned home with Moses, who had a bloodied nose and ripped shirt.

The police immediately laid a kidnapping charge. The following day, because the Benjamins were an established, well-known family, the story made bold headlines in all the prominent local newspapers.

Essie felt totally justified in having instigated the kidnapping. "He is my grandchild," she claimed. "I own him—he is more mine than yours! One day he will be my heir and continue the Benjamin name." She was well prepared for the baby's return to her home. A Chinese woman who recently lost her own infant still had an abundance of milk, and was engaged as a wet nurse to breastfeed my brother. It was common practice amongst many Chinese to employ wet nurses as surrogate mothers.

My desperate mother, accompanied by her sister Victoria for support, went to plead with her mother-in-law to return the baby. My grandmother turned on Victoria, who had been silent, saying, "And you take *this*," and punched her in the eye, leaving her with a painful black bruise!

During the following three months of separation from his mother, David was not nursing successfully. He had weighed little at birth, and now he was losing weight and gradually becoming ill, causing a great deal of anxiety and anguish in all members of both families.

The servants, relaying this distressing information to Liza, said, "He cly too muchee time, Missie Liza. Sleepie too little. They callee doctor many times. Say maybe nursee milk not enough."

Liza, powerless to act, and consumed with fear that her baby would not survive, was forced to await a judge's decision in the ruling British court. Chinese courts had no jurisdiction over foreign nationals enjoying extra-territoriality in the treaty ports.

# THE COURT CASE

On a hot, humid summer's day, the Benjamins and Jacobs, dressed in finery, arrived at the courthouse. Following the latest fashion dictates abroad, the women wore elegant outfits, gloves and hats, and the men wore stylish suits, top hats and spats. All sweated profusely, their anxiety adding to their discomfort. The folly of such unsuitable attire, in this land so distant from the cool European climes, was unquestionable.

Ceiling fans whirled in the courthouse, and intricately carved, fragrant, handheld sandalwood fans waved everywhere, in an effort to contain the insufferable heat. In the ensuing legal battle, the Judge awarded Liza custody with one proviso—she was to meet Benjy daily so he could see his son. Barely containing her fury, Essie sailed out of the courtroom, closely followed by her children, who were forbidden to acknowledge the Jacob family.

Every day without fail, Liza wheeled David in the stroller down Yu Yuen Road to meet Benjy in Jessfield Park. Eventually, without family interference, they relaxed and were able to converse with more ease. "The Judge was a very wise man," Mummy reflected. "He realized that forcing us to meet would probably lead to reconciliation. And it did in the end."

Benjy invited Liza to dinner at the romantic Rosemarie restaurant, where he had first proposed to her. She accepted his invitation with a degree of misgiving. Although at times she still missed him, she had started a secretarial job in a busy office and was slowly making a new life for herself.

The year apart had been extremely stressful and she feared a repetition of past events would lead to renewed and insurmountable difficulties. The incidence of divorce in the Sephardic community was extremely low, and social dictates were not easily ignored in the small, close-knit society.

An attractive, gifted young woman, Liza had always been popular, and once again attended dances and social events. She enjoyed playing tennis, badminton, and volleyball. She also set her mind and heart on successfully teaching herself to become a fancy diving champion, spending long hours in the heated YMCA swimming pool, on Bubbling Well Road. She would stand on the diving board facing the water, and—as always—saying 'die, die, live, live,' would fling herself out onto the water, at first landing flat on her back, but repeating this day after day until she finally mastered the dive called the *gainer*.

The lights were dim in the busy Rosemarie restaurant. Quiet-footed Chinese waiters faded into the background while the band played the beautiful strains of music from *The Merry Widow*. Benjy eloquently expressed his unwavering love for her, the emptiness and loneliness he experienced since her departure. "Come back to me, Liza darling, please come back. We'll start again in our own home, away from my mother's influence," he promised.

Finally, with some excitement, largely overshadowed by trepidation, Liza agreed to try again. "All right Benjy, I'll come back. But remember your promise to me—that we'll never go back to your mother's house." She hoped and prayed they were both wiser and better experienced to work things out and could put the difficult year behind them.

They moved into a tiny apartment on Yuen Ming Yuen Road. Difficult economic times surrounded the depression of 1929, and Benjy, along with many others, was unemployed, so Liza supported the home until he found a job selling radios. At the time, well-known brands included Philips and Blaupunkt. Passionate about the technology, he spent hours turning dials, and fine-tuning into stations few others could reach.

"In 1937 a big radio shop was going to open, so I applied," my father said.

"'Tell us—what do you know about this?' they asked. I said, 'I know how to handle salesmanship and I'm sure I'll make a success.' So, I got in, and in one month I sold six or seven radios!

"The manager said, 'Congratulations Benjamin—you did the best for the month!'

"I kept on going, going, going, until the end of 1937. I left in 1938, after they joined a giant company that asked why they should keep me on when they had their own people."

Gradually, my father re-ignited his career in real estate, gathering confidence from the realization that he had a natural talent for negotiating sales. "In time I did very nicely, and concluded many good deals," he said.

Adept at dealing with the Chinese and fully conversant in their language, he liked to relate how, sometimes, he was asked by an acquaintance he accidentally met on a street corner, to sell a certain property. "A short while later, not far away," Daddy said, "I sometimes met another acquaintance, and I told him about the new building just offered for sale. I followed my intuition."

A felicitous exchange, accompanied by smiles, nodding and bowing took place, followed by some negotiation and a final handshake. If conditions were acceptable, Benjy was close to finalizing a sale.

"In 1941," my father said, "my very big year came; it was thrown into my hands—by Eddie Hotung—when I was on my way to the synagogue on Saturday morning. He asked me, 'can you sell my father's property?'

"Which property is your father's? I asked. He said, 'Huge property in Hongkew. Four roads—a whole square. All big houses, shops and all.'

"I was very excited! I said, Eddie—on Monday morning, I will come to you. Give me your details, of rents and everything else. So I got it all, and went straight down to the people who were asking for big properties. I asked them, 'Do you know who the owner is?' They all knew the property very well, and said, 'Yes sure—Hotung.' I put them together—and did the deal. Two million dollars!"

"Two million dollars!" My father stunned me with the amount.

"Yes," he said. "Two brokers—and I was one of the two."

"Right. And how much was your commission?" I asked.

"$25,000—half-half." He answered, smiling at the exciting memory.

"Daddy," I said, "in those days that was a huge sum of money! Do you remember what the average monthly rent was?" I was really keen to know every detail.

"No, I don't remember—very big rent," he said. "Thousands and thousands of dollars. Big shops…"

For a short while after the court case, the relationship with Essie was strained. Benjy resolutely refused further domination by his mother. Eventually, she reconciled to her son's separate existence and invited them to share Sabbath and festival meals. Huge platters of delicious aromatic food, including Saffron yellow rice dotted with raisins, mutton curry, rice and semolina dumplings, and various special traditional Sephardic culinary favorites, were brought to the table in a steady stream. Each additional dish appeared to be the one that would certainly take the table down in a crashing crescendo.

These long, savored dinners were followed by after meal prayers, recited in a singsong manner. On any occasion but the Sabbath or days of religious observance, the men would smoke cigars and pipes and discuss business, politics, the races, and the stock exchange.

Benjy, Liza, Ester, David, circ 1939

The ladies spoke of forthcoming celebrations and the latest fashion trends. They complained about, or praised their servants, spoke of visits to the doctor, exchanged recipes, and sometimes played cards. They shared tidbits of community gossip while servants cleared everything from the tables and restored the household to its usual good order.

Silently and unobtrusively, the staff eavesdropped, and wasted no time relating interesting information to servants in surrounding households. In this way, many family secrets were spilled, and a number of long-lasting family feuds were generated.

It was into this ambience that I was born in 1937. I was named Estelle, after my grandmother, Essie, whose real name was Esther. I found it enigmatic that neither of us ever used our real names. I was nicknamed Ester, with a middle name of Rosemary, memorializing the restaurant where Daddy proposed to Mummy, and where, in shy response, she had momentarily slipped under the table before emerging to accept.

# THE BATTLE FOR SHANGHAI

With the outbreak of the second Sino-Japanese war, in 1937, massive trouble was brewing in Shanghai. Fights between the Chinese and Japanese had, until then, been referred to, and described as, "incidents."

In July, the Japanese had expanded their fleet of warships to more than twenty, and moved them down the Whampu. Provocatively, they moored their warship, *Idzumo*, directly in front of the International Settlement, where it was clearly visible from Nanking Road and the Cathay Hotel. They declared total authority over Hongkew. They thought they would defeat the Chinese and take possession of Shanghai within a week or two, but encountered a fight and bravery that both astonished and enraged them. The Chinese resistance won the admiration and respect of the whole world, including their enemies!

On August 13, sporadic firing between the sides struck terror into thousands of Chinese, who still held fresh memories of the 1932 bombings. They began streaming towards the "security" of the foreign settlements, as yet untouched by the Japanese.

In the afternoon of August 14, tragedy struck and pandemonium broke out, when 550lb bombs were erroneously unleashed on the crowded intersection of The Bund and Nanking Road, one of them striking and demolishing the upper stories of the Palace Hotel, killing a large number of people, and another landing in Nanking Road between the Palace and Cathay Hotels, in the International Settlement. Soon after, two more misdirected bombs were unleashed on Avenue Edward VII. Altogether, thousands of innocent victims of all nationalities, many of them women and children, were killed and injured.

The day became indelibly known as "Black," or, "Bloody Saturday."

An acquaintance of ours was one of many people who stood on the roof of the Cathay Hotel and watched, horrified, as perilously close aircraft dispensed their deadly, misplaced loads on unsuspecting, innocent victims below. "We saw shells flying overhead," he related, "and heard the thunderous crashing of the bombs as they landed. We got out of there as fast as our legs could carry us!"

Ironically, the Chinese were unintentionally responsible for firing the bombs that caused the appalling carnage and misery, and reduced buildings to rubble. Their intended target, hopelessly missed with devastating consequences, was the Japanese warship *Idzumo*, loaded with munitions, that later sank the British warship, *HMS Peterel*.

Grotesquely distorted, dismembered bodies, severed body parts and limbs, even heads, were randomly strewn about. People lay bleeding and dying. Many, seriously injured, crawled into side-alleys to die. Some poor, confused souls staggered around in the chaos, hands held to their heads, calling out names in a vain search for missing friends and loved ones. Screams and cries rent the air.

Cars and trams were mangled and set ablaze, burning trapped occupants to cinders. Rickshaws, pedicabs, bicycles, and other conveyances, lay crushed and partially buried under the rubble of fallen cement and shattered glass.

The foreign enclaves were flooded with a steady deluge of thousands of panic-stricken Chinese refugees fleeing from neighboring Chapei and Kiangwan—leaving homes largely devastated by Japanese and Chinese shelling. The lines of people stretched for miles—some were several generations of the same family, helping, carrying, and holding onto each other. They crossed Garden Bridge, the only open access, in a frenzied stampede, slipping and falling, trampling already crushed bodies underfoot, in their maddened determination to reach the International Settlement.

Thousands of homeless souls were accommodated wherever possible. Camps were set up to inoculate them against disease, and to distribute small, watery rations of rice gruel. Multitudes slept on the sidewalks, streets, in alleyways and parks. The unbearable August heat compounded the misery.

Corpses were appearing on the streets in ever growing numbers as death took its hold. In some districts they lay exposed in the sizzling sun for days, seriously menacing the living. Most often these were small babies, hundreds of which were picked up daily by The Chinese Benevolent Society. The tiny bundles were visible everywhere on the streets—infants—wrapped in straw matting, paper, and rags. Some were shoved into trashcans!

Dense clouds of smoke hung over large stricken areas of Shanghai, making breathing difficult. Nightly, the sky was alight with a fiery red glow.

The British authorities issued an evacuation order, and instructed all nationals wishing to leave to assemble and register in the Shanghai Club.

Four days after "Bloody Saturday," on August 18th, they shipped the first load of evacuees, between 1300 and 1500 nationals—mainly women and children—out of harm's way to Hong Kong. Amongst them were several Canadians and Americans.

*Empress of Asia* evacuated Liza to Hong Kong in 1937 during the Battle for Shanghai. Photo courtesy Nelson Oliver.

The evacuees travelled ten miles by frail tender, downriver to the sea, at Woosung. There they embarked on a specifically commandeered ship, *Empress of Asia*, that had just brought several hundred members of the Royal Ulster Rifles from Hong Kong to complement the British garrison at Shanghai. To identify the *Empress* as non-combatant, The Union Jack was painted on the deck and hull.

My mother was an evacuee on that ship. My father remained behind in Shanghai.

The vessel was excessively overloaded with about 400 passengers—many lived and slept on the crowded decks for the three-day journey.

"I was repatriated during the troubles in 1937," Mummy said, referring to the escalating Sino-Japanese fight for control. "The British sent mothers—women and children—to Hong Kong. I took my little baby,

David, in my arms—and I was already several months pregnant with you… we slept on a deckchair. People were sleeping on the floor, and anywhere they could find space. How I longed to be in a cabin."

My father's mother, and four of his siblings were all evacuees on another ship. Unable to secure cabin accommodation, they slept wherever they could place themselves on the deck. In Hong Kong, my mother shared their large room in a big brick building at the racecourse, in Happy Valley. When they returned to Shanghai a few weeks later, she remained behind and moved to another place.

After "Bloody Saturday" Shanghai was panic-stricken! Big banks along the Bund, fearing for the safety of customers and staff, closed their doors. Shop fronts were boarded up, business came to a virtual standstill, and money and food were almost unobtainable. Several thousand more British and Americans were evacuated. Shiploads of insightful foreigners departed for different ports—including Manila and Japan. Even wealthy Chinese were shifting themselves, and their wealth, to Hong Kong.

As the initial panic wore off, Shanghai once again began to assume a degree of normalcy. Business resumed and shops re-opened their doors—with misplaced optimism. On August 23, an unidentified aircraft dropped two bombs on the center of the International Settlement. One failed to detonate, and the other struck Wing On Department Store on Nanking Road, once again tragically killing and wounding hundreds.

In the ensuing months, countless thousands of Chinese continued to pour into the settlements, stretching resources to breaking point. As fighting escalated, more deadly bombs continued to kill innocent victims and destroy landmarks. The Japanese deliberately chose to bomb Shanghai South Station at a time when it was crowded with refugees.

"Where did you stay when you left Happy Valley?" I asked my mother.

"There was a two-storey place on the mountain called 'The Castle'—a hundred-year-old place—the British put us all over there, in the clubhouse."

"Oh—all?" I exclaimed. "There were so many?"

"No—we were just a few British-Jewish families in the castle. We all looked after each other. During that time there was a tremendous typhoon, and I was with my baby, *and* pregnant! The roof flew up and down—it was terrifying—and they quickly called us all downstairs. The place was shaking as we descended. Everyone sat under a very wide staircase—and in the morning they came to see who was still alive!"

"Oh my God! And were some people hurt?" I was astonished by this new information.

"Nothing much, really—just a little bit of something fell on someone," she said vaguely. "The castle withstood it—a one-hundred-year-old, beautiful place. We had wonderful food—they provided very good Chinese cooks. During the day I often walked up and down the mountain. The views were magnificent. I was very fit—I loved it."

My aunt Victoria's family, fearing for their safety during the fighting, had relocated permanently to Hong Kong several months earlier. "And also," Mummy told me, "they found it hard to make a living in Shanghai. Business was slowly deteriorating during that period—worse and worse and worse. It was during the Depression—it had already started quite a while before we got married in 1935. People were doing away with themselves long before, all over the world."

It was very comforting for my mother, nearing the end of her pregnancy, to have her sister nearby. She had a lively toddler to care for, and feared for my father's safety in Shanghai.

"Which hospital was I born in?"

"The *Matilda*. I was taken there in the early hours of morning, in terrible agony! Every little while I was having contractions, and the woman who went with me—Mrs. Cohen—was helping, and trying to hold me… and oh—the pain was awful! And the poor chauffeur didn't know where to go. Imagine—he lost his way and was going round in circles, higher and higher! It was *dark* on the mountain, with narrow winding roads. Poor Mrs. Cohen was saying, 'Oh, oh!' And I said that I don't want to give birth in the car! I was so afraid…" Mummy laughed.

"Oh my goodness!" I exclaimed, feeling certain it was no laughing matter at the time.

"Can you imagine what a terrible time? At last, we got to the hospital! It was already almost morning when they took me, quickly put me on the bed, and started preparing me at full speed. Just in time! You were born at around 7:30 in the morning. I stayed there several days longer than usual, because there were no adequate facilities for a newborn baby in the castle. Daddy was still in Shanghai. He came after you were born, and we all returned when you were about three months old."

I never knew my mother had stayed in an old castle on the island for so many months. Had I known when I revisited Hong Kong in 1987, I would have attempted to find the place, if it still existed. I don't recall her ever mentioning it during the years we lived there, after the war.

In 1955, *Love is a Many Splendored Thing*, the movie starring William Holden and Jennifer Jones, was filmed in the Matilda Hospital. It was the first time I saw the place, albeit on screen, where I was delivered into the world. It was both an exciting and emotionally evocative experience for me.

# NANKING

In December 1937, driven by rage and resentment at the fierce resistance of the Chinese troops—led by General Chiang Kai-shek in the Battle of Shanghai—50,000 Japanese soldiers, bent on exacting savage revenge, marched into Nanking. The Shanghai battle had lasted throughout the summer until November, negating their empty boast that they would conquer all of China within three months.

Chinese soldiers at Nanking, in contrast with Shanghai, greatly outnumbered the Japanese; they had sufficient ammunition—but were largely disorganized and lacked cohesive leadership. After just four days of fighting, the Chinese, cowed by the enemy's ferocious attack, beat a disorderly retreat. The Japanese were ordered to 'kill all captives,' and to eliminate any threat from the estimated 90,000 Chinese soldiers who surrendered.

In the ensuing weeks of carnage that became known as *The Rape of Nanking*, the Japanese murdered half the population of 600,000 civilians and soldiers in the city. They proceeded to rape and plunder on an unimaginable scale, striking terror and inflicting insurmountable agony on the inhabitants of the invaded city. No one, old or young, was spared.

Chinese POWs were trucked to remote outskirts of the city. There, young soldiers, encouraged by their superiors, inflicted maximum pain and suffering—conducting bayonet practice on individual captives. They held contests to see who could decapitate the most Chinese, and smiled proudly while displaying their victims' heads strung up on a line.

Gasoline-soaked, bound and trussed up prisoners were burned alive, and others, perhaps more fortunately, were simply mowed down by machine-guns. Some victims were strangled and drowned. They killed storeowners, and after looting shops they mercilessly locked people inside and set buildings on fire, deriving pleasure from watching people desperately trying to escape—even by jumping off rooftops!

Chinese dug their own graves, and some were forced to bury others alive. The merciless aggressors, desensitized to human suffering, posed triumphantly for photographs beside mutilated bodies.

Next the Japanese soldiers focused their attention on the women—old and young—sparing none from their animalistic sexual abuse, not even pregnant women. In many instances, after being raped, their bellies were slit open and their fetuses ripped out!

An estimated number of no less than 20,000 gang-raped women—some reports put the figure as high as 80,000—were bayoneted or shot, so they could never bear witness to the atrocities.

Sometimes Chinese men and their sons were forced to rape their own daughters, mothers, and sisters, while the rest of the devastated family was made to watch the ignominy.

Bloodthirsty soldiers shot anyone on a whim, and frequently fired randomly into crowds, killing civilians indiscriminately—further terrorizing, traumatizing, and spreading panic throughout Nanking.

The massive citywide destruction and slaughter continued without cease for about six weeks, until the beginning of February 1938. Corpses—some piled high—lay everywhere. The streets of Nanking ran red with blood!

Following the initial, unprecedented carnage, the Japanese attempted to pacify the decimated population by distributing highly addictive opium and heroin to people of all ages. Tens of thousands became addicted to the narcotics, many losing themselves in opium dens.

For their sole sexual pleasure, the Japanese introduced the notorious Comfort Women—that forced youthful Chinese women into slave-prostitution.

Any victory of the Imperial Army, large or small, was celebrated by Japan, whose only goal—regardless of the extreme suffering and sacrifice of others—was the expansion and glory of the Japanese empire.

My parents had not, as yet, returned to Shanghai from Hong Kong while the foregoing carnage was taking place in Nanking. Eventually some of the news of the horrifying events filtered through, but it would be many years before the full extent of the Japanese atrocities would become known. Even then, much information was probably lost because of their practice of murdering victims who may possibly bear witness and eventually testify in a war crimes tribunal.

A small number of remarkably altruistic Americans and Europeans—doctors, businessmen, and missionaries—remained in Nanking. Flouting the Japanese, they bravely established a 2.5 square mile International Safety Zone in the middle of the city, using Red Cross flags as the "off limits" demarcation line.

These unsung heroes constantly risked their lives when intervening on behalf of Chinese men about to be executed, or preventing the rape of women and young girls.

We have them to thank for their daily, meticulous recording of the atrocities they witnessed, which they described as "Hell on earth, and cruel beyond measure."

During the Rape of Nanking about 300,000 Chinese took shelter inside the safety zone, and almost all who did not make it into the zone ultimately perished.

## AUNTIE SALLY

Daddy's sister, Auntie Sally, lived on the ground floor in the same three-section apartment complex as ours, on Nan Yang Road. We ran freely in and out of her home when needing a glass of water or quick pee. Each section had its own entrance, shared an adjoining wall, and faced the long narrow garden, which ran the whole length of the building. We lived in the third entrance on the right, facing the splendid magnolia tree. Her apartment, in the first entrance, was easily accessible and welcoming, making the distance upstairs to our home too horrible to contemplate when we were having fun and didn't want to skip a beat in our games. After school hours we spent most lazy summer days playing in the garden with our cousins, Tony and David.

Many stray cats and dogs lived in our neighborhood and, for some obscure reason, found our garden and the adjoining one extremely desirable as a playing field and public bathroom—perhaps because we were guilty of feeding them. I loved animals and unfortunately could not refrain from playing with these strays. Each time I was scratched or bitten I had to go to the hospital for anti-rabies injections. Horrible long needles were injected into my little stomach. When I was lucky enough to be bitten by an identified pet I only had to endure ten shots if the quarantine animal was clear of rabies. Unfortunately, most of my mishaps were with stray animals, which meant I was in for the full twenty. I was very brave and always resigned myself to this punishment, which I endured at least five times in my youth.

A white cat arrived one day through the window at the side of the house, at the top of the stairs. It must have performed some very intricate maneuvers over adjoining rooftops and gutters in order to get to our window, the furthermost one in the entire complex. He just stood staring at us for a while. We stared back, transfixed by the sheer beauty of this new arrival, a large, apparently highly-bred Persian. We hardly dared to breathe fearing he would leave again, but after summing us up for a few minutes, the cat walked haughtily past, clearly intending to take up permanent residence in our home.

Allowing us to follow him when we kept a suitable distance between us, His Majesty, the Cat, embarked on an investigative tour of our apartment. He sailed from room to room and into the enclosed balcony, sitting down for a few moments in various spots, as if testing each for suitability as a resting place. During these moments, we too were expected to come to a standstill until the cat was up and moving again.

We named him Beauty, and before long he allowed us to pet and play with him. Very soon we were fighting for possession and a turn to play with Beauty. "This cat is mine," David claimed. "I am the oldest, so I should have first choice." I knew what *that* meant. No more marbles or soccer if I disagreed, so I deferred, hoping that he would soon be bored with this new diversion and go back to climbing the magnolia tree.

Beauty enjoyed this excessive attention for a while but then, fed-up, he taught us a lesson by suddenly exiting through the same window from which he had made his entry. Devastated, we spent hours vainly searching the surrounding areas calling his name and holding out tempting bits of food. Finally, convinced he was gone forever, we gave up and returned home. Three days later he re-entered through the window and reclaimed his throne. We were soon to find out these disappearances would be repeated at irregular intervals. Beauty appeared to revel in the attention lavished on him when he returned.

Some time after Beauty's arrival, a neighbor's cat had a litter that bore an uncanny resemblance to our own princely cat. I think Beauty probably sired many gorgeous kittens during his sudden forays into the night. There was always a lot of yowling and meowing at night around our building.

All signs of mice disappeared and we didn't have to set out any more traps at night. One day, while I was doing homework, Beauty rushed into the room with a large mouse dangling from his mouth. He had come to show us how proud he was of himself!

"Go away Beauty, go away!" I shrieked, and promptly jumped onto a nearby chair. Offended, Beauty immediately leapt up to join me on the small, unoccupied space beside my feet. He couldn't understand why I wasn't praising him! Disgusted, he dropped the lifeless mouse, departed in a hurry, and was nowhere to be seen for a few hours.

Amah, when summoned to dispose of the prey, laughed hysterically to see me still standing and shaking on the chair. She took her time removing the rodent, and for a long while after the incident, was heard relating the story between choking fits of laughter to all of her visiting friends.

## AMAH

I never knew where Amah went on her day off from work. She occupied a little room in the servants' quarters of the house, and always seemed to be available when needed. She, and all other household help, could be summoned at any time to do the smallest of chores for the lazy, privileged population. Even a glass of water was delivered to us on an elegant silver tray.

Sometimes she entertained a friend in her room and I was always welcome to join them. I watched, fascinated, as they used silk or cotton threads to skillfully "tweak" each other's unwanted facial and bodily hair. Known as "threading," the ancient art is thought to have originated in Turkey—but China, India, and parts of the Middle East also claim to have been first to practice it. It looked painful. Amah and her friend pulled faces and made small grunting sounds as they were "tweaked." Smooth skin was very desirable, so they endured their discomfort stoically!

When we were very young, under the age of seven or eight, Amah always accompanied us to the school bus stop, or to small nearby shops, to purchase tasty treats. I held her hand tightly all the way to the stores, my mouth watering in anticipation of what awaited us there. Jars full of candy, cookies, and dried Chinese plums and fruit were everywhere, and delicious vanilla ice cream and lemonade were in the ice chests. It was a difficult choice to purchase just one item because we had so little extra spending money.

In my favorite store, Mr. Wu usually looked up from his abacus to greet me, before returning to work on his calculations. "Hello you, Missee Esta," he would say peering above his wire-rimmed spectacles. "You takee something nice today?" I watched in fascination as his fingers flew up and down, moving the counters strung on parallel rods in the large, shiny black wooden frame.

I think Amah liked him a lot. We always lingered a long time in Mr. Wu's store, and Amah kept looking at him from the corner of her eye. Sometimes he stopped calculating, and chatted with her for a while, after which she stayed in a good mood for a long time, occasionally allowing a secret smile to crease her usually inscrutable features.

Quite often, Amah would hail a bicycle-driven pedicab, or rickshaw, pulled by a sweaty, running man, who was generally barefoot or wearing rope sandals, scantily dressed in ragged clothing, and often bare from the waist up. Suddenly, miraculously, several conveyances would arrive together, the drivers jostling each other, their loud voices creating a din. Pedicabs were more spacious and usually cleaner than rickshaws.

A rickshaw puller had not much more to look forward to other than the stretch of road ahead. Once caught in the miserable cycle of hand-to-mouth existence, he had little hope of elevating himself to an improved lifestyle and better living conditions. Through a number of adverse circumstances, perhaps losing his previous job, he might have been forced to become a rickshaw-man, working shifts with one or two others. Large companies owned the rickshaws and rented them to sub-contractors. They, in turn, rented them to coolies, who, from their meager earnings, had to pay for traffic fines and repairs. Contractors, who suspected them of hiding some of their earnings, abused them. Towering, red-turbaned Sikh policemen in the International Settlement regularly clubbed them for minor traffic offences.

Those seriously endangered, undernourished, and overworked men suffered from a multitude of diseases—malnutrition, tuberculosis, cholera, typhoid, leprosy and other indigenous ailments. They had a shortened lifespan of about thirty years.

Obviously enjoying and prolonging her moment of power, Amah always bargained loudly with her countrymen for the best fare before climbing awkwardly aboard the chosen vehicle with us. She viewed them as inferior coolies, happily observing the caste code that placed her above them on the Chinese scale of importance. This provoked some rickshaw pullers into spitting disdainfully and carefully on the ground, close to

Amah's black cloth shoe, as she boarded the conveyance.

Sometimes we would go for a walk in the neighborhood, with or without Amah. I always stopped to watch and listen to the Chinese man near our home who walked around playing the *Huqin*—pronounced something like *wu-chin*—a bowed instrument with very few strings, from which he managed to eke out some miserable, reedy music. His shoulders and back were strung with instruments for sale to locals, or tourists—as a curious memento of their China visit. The Chinese bargained loudly for the best price, and sometimes, considering the large number of *huqins* he carried, he didn't appear to have made many sales. How could he support a family with such meager earnings?

Any casual stroll revealed the excitement and sadness of everyday life in Shanghai, the city of extremes. Without real comprehension, we knew that the inevitable bundles we daily saw on doorsteps were baby girls, abandoned by distraught parents without resources. Sometimes daughters were sold for cash to good-time madams, and worse, stories were whispered of avoiding bad luck times by murdering female progeny.

Chinese mothers loved their daughters but avoided closeness that eventually caused great pain when the daughter married and moved in with her husband's family, where she was bound in service to her new clan. Her mother was never welcome in her new home—because she would be too sentimental, and disrupt the mother-in-law's dominance. Mothers preferred sons, who married and brought girls into *their* homes to do their bidding and support them in their old age.

I don't know how we came by the knowledge of life and death on the streets. I suspect we overheard adults or Amah speak of the sights, and in some way the sheer volume of misery we saw each day immunized us.

Disfigured lepers, with hideously distorted, destroyed features, were ubiquitous, striking terror into superstitious passersby. Lice-infested beggars lined the streets, scratching themselves incessantly, and picking vermin off their own, and each other's bodies—to little, or no avail. Some had been deliberately maimed and crippled by their own families to generate a source of income.

Sometimes we saw a body that had finally succumbed to disease or to the harsh, hostile living conditions. Once, in winter, Mummy saw two small dead boys lying on the sidewalk. They were clothed in rags, painfully thin, and completely frozen. Their poverty stricken parents, barely existing in the interior, had sent them into the city to beg... tins lay beside their rigid bodies that would soon be collected, along with many others, by the

Chinese Benevolent Society.

While walking on a narrow backstreet when she was a young girl, Mummy saw a pregnant Chinese woman squat suddenly to deliver her own baby on the sidewalk. She laid out a ragged blanket she had been carrying, and after a few cries and grunts, gave birth! She was surrounded almost instantly by passersby, and soon disappeared from sight with her bundled-up infant!

We were really rather curious to encounter fresh situations each time we set out, even though at a young age we seemed to take everything in stride. Anything seemed possible in Shanghai!

Extreme swings in climate, or more often, infection from drinking water and contaminated food, were a real danger to those poor souls who lived on the filthy streets. We only drank boiled water, and all fruit and vegetables were soaked in water that turned a gorgeous purple when some Permanganate of Potash, a disinfectant, was added to it. The Chinese fertilized their fields with human waste—the night soil—collected daily, in what were ironically called *honey pots*.

Every year we were inoculated against cholera and typhoid. Yellow Jaundice was one of the other perils that befell many. As children, we all had bouts of it—it was common for our ever-vigilant mother to check our eyes and urine for signs of yellowing. Stomach worms appeared from time-to-time, as did ringworm. One of us always had some part of ourselves painted red, purple or yellow, from Mercurochrome, Gentian Violet, or yellow Iodine, the usual treatments of the day for minor injuries. Sulfadiazine was frequently mentioned and administered as the probable cure for any bacterial infection.

Annual winter chilblains, caused by exposure to cold and damp conditions, were common. Sometimes I scratched my unbearably itchy, swollen feet until they bled.

On the Sabbath, in accordance with strict observance regarding the handling of money on the day of rest, payment for conveyance was made with previously purchased tokens.

Daddy's car stood idle on the Sabbath, but on Sundays and sometimes during the week, we loved going for a ride. We were privileged to own the shiny black Packard that smelt of leather. When I think back on those days I can almost remember the special strong scent of the leather of yesteryear. I think early childhood experiences are stored somewhere in memory, and in recall, evoke the strongest feelings of nostalgia.

Often, we passed a dwelling that had scaffolding on the side of it. When a Chinese person died, a bamboo scaffold was immediately built alongside the building to remove the body through the window so the spirit wasn't left to hover around inside forever. You could actually go around the block, and by the time you returned the scaffolding would be up—that's how fast they worked! The workers could run up and down the thin rungs with breathtaking sure-footedness!

I remember Daddy's car breaking down in one of Shanghai's many wonderful leafy lanes, and the effort he put into getting it started again. We all piled out and stood waiting noisily while he cranked the car. But we didn't mind—it seemed very exciting and adventurous, really. Even encountering a funeral procession and being held up for a lengthy period until the last row passed, was exciting and interesting.

In a Chinese funeral, the size of the procession depended on the importance of the person who died. A wealthy family could "rent a crying crowd" that cried and wailed loudly. Sometimes brass-band musicians, wearing smart uniforms and tall hats with ostrich plumes, heralded the funeral. In front of the procession of mourners, you would see a large framed photograph of the deceased, either carried aloft, or as the single occupant of the back seat of a car. It was often decked with floral garlands. This was followed by a sedan chair carrying a wife, mother, or other important female family member who, completely hidden by curtains, never showed her face. As a token of humility, close relatives were clothed entirely in garments of roughest white cloth that distinguished them from other mourners. Following them were distant relatives, friends and business acquaintances. The last people in the procession were the paid professionals, who threw themselves into frenzied grief. The larger the rented crowd, the more effective was the wailing, lamenting and crying, indicating how much the deceased was loved and would be missed. It acknowledged the tragic family loss and was an attempt to slow down the departure of the spirit into the next world.

Sometimes a huge, seemingly endless procession collected a large number of curious street people on the way that tagged along purely for the fun of being part of it all, and hopeful of receiving food, candy, and lucky coins wrapped in white paper.

# MOSQUITO NETS

Every night Daddy gathered up the huge, heavy mosquito nets that hung from a ring in the ceiling above our beds, and fanning them out like a tent, he tucked the nets under our mattresses. While swarms of banished, bloodthirsty mosquitoes hummed hopefully, and buzzed wildly around the netting, looking for some tiny re-entryway, we said our prayers before going to sleep. "*Sh'ma Yisrael*—Hear, Oh Israel" we recited in unison, always following these ancient words with "God bless Mummy and Daddy, Granny and Grandpa, all my uncles and aunts and cousins, and brother and sister."

Occasionally, though many years have passed, I surprise myself by suddenly reverting to my childhood prayers, automatically including relatives who are no longer with us. When this happens, my senses are flooded with nostalgia, and for a brief moment I am once again that little Ester, vulnerable and trusting, as yet untouched by the vicissitudes of life. Now, decades later, I am Mummy, Grandma and Auntie, hoping for my own inclusion in someone's prayers.

It has been my lifelong habit to slip under the bed covers, always completely covering my head before falling asleep. With sudden insight, I understand that the reason for this strange behavior stemmed from those early days under the mosquito net, when I would hear the dreaded hum and feel the light brush of an infiltrator as it settled on my young, tender, and as yet unlined face.

Shanghai, so full of dirty creeks and waterways, was a most fertile breeding ground for Malaria and other serious diseases. Many unwelcome bugs thrived in the hot and humid summer climate, emerging at night and running riot in our home. Not least of these were huge, hungry flying cockroaches, which zoomed in through windows, settling everywhere and foraging for food. The servants trapped them in a large innovative trapping bottle, set on the kitchen counter each night. I never asked, nor did I wish to know, what they did with the daily bounty, the jarful of ugly, crawling, frantically flapping cockroaches they collected every morning.

At night, it seemed as if countless crickets from the four corners of earth were in the gardens below, creating a noisy, tuneless din. With the advent of dawn, busy neighborhood birds chirped for a while. Then the rest of a lazy summer's day belonged to the rulers of the trees, the Cicadas, otherwise known to us as "Scissor-grinders." I was always spellbound when my brother David, holding one, stopped and started its grinding sound by pressing and releasing some secret spot on the creature.

David got Cicadas out of the magnolia tree, which dominated the garden in front of our apartment. He was constantly climbing and disappearing behind the lush branches and beautiful white magnolias of the handsome tree, which equaled the height of our building. I longed to follow him to the upper branches but, being a little girl, two years his junior, I only managed to clamber onto the lowest large branch, where I would freeze from fright. David would look down from his lofty position and rescue me after I promised to perform some chore, such as climbing several flights to our apartment to bring him food and water. He built a tree house from odd bits of wood and cardboard, emulating "Tarzan," for whom, to the best of my knowledge, no "Jane" ever appeared. I felt dejected when our cousin, Tony, was sometimes invited to the upper branches to share a treat.

One day, David fell out of the tree and broke his toe. "Get Mummy," he cried, thankful Daddy wasn't home yet from work, and scared of being punished for climbing too high. After scolding David, Mummy filled him up with more self-importance by lavishing extra attention on him. Unlike Daddy, who had been an over-sheltered child, Mummy had an adventurous nature, attempting all kinds of difficult feats.

The tree climbing ended for a short while, so we played marbles and ball games instead. When his toe healed, I was only permitted to play football if I agreed to be the goalkeeper. Eagerly, I agreed to any condition in exchange for the dubious privilege of being "one of the boys."

Sometimes, while waiting for David to descend from his kingdom in the branches I amused myself by digging in the soil around the base of the tree. I was searching for bits of *Jos*—good luck and prayer tokens—left there by Chinese who lived and worked around us. These bits and pieces usually included coins, some written notes, *Jos* sticks, or incense, burnt in offering to the Gods and ancestors. The Chinese revere and worship their ancestors and continue to respect them through the generations. I imagined all kinds of mystical situations and wondered who had left those fresh deposits, and whether their prayers were being answered.

I loved the magical world and was thrilled one day to find a car aerial lying in the street. This immediately became a magic wand, which I waved about while standing on my bed, muttering "Abracadabra," and some other forgotten incantations. Finally, I jumped off, always believing and hoping I would suddenly be able to fly. My little sister, Sylvia, three years my junior, would watch me wide-eyed with expectancy, clapping and laughing after each flying jump. Regularly, David and I fashioned her perambulator into a rickshaw and ran her up and down the length of our verandah, enjoying her alternating squeals of delight and terror!

Daddy regaled my siblings and me for hours with stories of his childhood. He spoke of a house full of ever-present Chinese Amahs and Japanese servants waiting on their slightest bidding. Creature comforts were taken care of and they luxuriated in the general lifestyle of privileged foreigners and wealthy Chinese.

He had a captive audience in us, with tales of primitive surgical operations and procedures in the early part of the twentieth century. Mummy hovered on the fringes, smiling faintly. It was certain she had heard these stories over and over again.

"Once," Daddy said, "I fell and grazed my knee so badly, it soon became swollen and infected. In order to treat it, the doctors soaked my leg in hot water until the skin was softened, and then they peeled it off, layer after layer, until they reached the area of infection to medicate it." He loved to relate this horrific event, which he assured us had to be repeated a number of times. Using creative sound effects and vivid descriptions, he evoked wide-eyed shock on our little faces. Perhaps this justified the extent of his agony during those barbaric serial procedures.

Daddy loved to tease and bully his sisters. "When my sisters were very little and taking a bath," he said, "I would slip a small piece of pink soap into the water and tell them someone's little toe had come off." Convinced, they howled inconsolably until their Amah came to the rescue.

When I was a child, during the Japanese occupation in the early days of World War II, taking a bath was not always a simple matter—there was no running hot water, so boiling bathwater had to be ordered from a special place. Very often I accompanied Daddy to the bathhouse to order hot water to be delivered at a specific time. Several Chinese men were employed to stoke and take care of the stoves. The boiling water created an unbearably hot and steamy environment. Conversing in fluent Chinese, Daddy placed the order and paid for the delivery. At the agreed time a Chinese coolie, chanting "hey-ho, hey-ho," would arrive, with two barrels full of boiling water hanging from each end of a bamboo pole carried across his shoulder. With great skill, he had run all the way through crowded streets and up four flights of steps, without spilling a drop!


Every day, at around one o'clock, Daddy came home for *tiffin*, an Anglo-Indian word for lunch, or light meal. He always went to work in a suit, but removed his jacket and tie as soon as he returned home. During intensely hot summer days he used a large white handkerchief to mop the sweat dripping from his brow, face, and neck. Everyone perspired profusely, and, whenever possible, wore very light clothing. Sometimes, when playing, we only wore shorts and *singlets* (vests.)

In many dwellings, during mealtimes, a large *punkah*, hanging from the ceiling, was still widely employed to combat the relentless heat. This was an eight to ten-foot long frame, around three feet in height, which was covered with white cloth. A rope, attached to it like a bell-pull, was fed through a hole in the wall into the next room. There, a servant pulled, and kept the *punkah* in perpetual motion, diffusing a constant stream of cool air.

There was no limit to the number of innovative ways, menial and bestial, in which Chinese were employed to gratify and perpetuate the comforts of the privileged people of Shanghai.

## AUNTIE EILEEN

When I was five-years-old, Mummy introduced her friend, Joseph Feller, to my father's youngest sister, Eileen. Joe and my mother were members of *Betar*, a Zionist youth movement. Mummy took Eileen to the campsite where he was spending the weekend and asked someone to call him. Joe was very tall, so he ducked down to step out of the huge tent. When he stood up and saw Eileen, also tall and very pretty, he was transfixed. They just stared at each other for a long while.

"It was love at first sight—the most romantic moment," my mother said. "Everyone watched them fall instantly in love—I just knew they were made for each other."

Auntie Eileen was so happy. "I'm getting married, and you're going to be my flower girl, would you like that, Darling? We're going to the tailor to make a pretty dress for you," she told me. I loved her so much—she was always hugging and cuddling me. I could hardly eat or sleep from excitement, waiting for the day we were going to the Chinese tailor shop. She picked me up and we rode in a pedicab to a bustling, busy *lilong*, an alley, where we got off and walked to the tailor. We entered a jam-packed room, where several Chinese were sewing by hand and on machines.

"This is my niece, Ester," she told the owner, who approached us immediately. He knew my aunt, and smiled, nodding his head and bowing in greeting. "She is going to be my flower girl. We want you to make a beautiful dress for her. Handmade."

They focused all their attention on me, making me feel very special and important. We looked through a huge array of hanging and folded fabrics, in every available color and texture, and finally selected beautiful blue velvet. I held it to my face—it felt so soft.

"You likee this one, little Missee? I makee you velly pletty dless," the tailor said. Auntie Eileen nodded assent, "Sure Darling—you can have this one if you love it."

After discussing styles and paging through a fashion book, the tailor stood me on a table and took my measurements. "You comee back tomollow, you tly on. One day after—I finish dless," he said, bowing.

I wore the beautiful long dress he made, especially for me, to the wedding at Ohel Rachel Synagogue. The velvet seemed to be alive, changing hues of blue as I moved around under the lights. I was so happy.

It was December 1942, the middle of a freezing Shanghai winter, during the very difficult time preceding the internment of most of our family members.

Auntie Eileen's pending internment at Yangchow camp was looming. Joe, being Russian, was not interned. The day came when they were wrenched apart, and would remain separated for almost three years—until the end of the war, when they could eventually "resume" being married.

# THE ZETZA FAMILY

"Come in. Come in children." Smiling broadly, and speaking in a deep voice with a heavy Polish accent, Mr. Zetza welcomes us into his home directly beneath our apartment.

Mrs. Zetza stands beside him, wiping her hands on her apron while nodding and smiling agreeably at us. She has chubby, pink cheeks and short, wispy grey hair. "Come in children," she echoes, "and have a little something nice to eat."

This is a prearranged ritual that is often repeated when Mummy is displeased with us for some wrongdoing or bad behavior. "You must leave home," she would say, and the three of us, exiled, would descend one flight on the short distance to rescue. The Zetzas are both short and tubby with persistently benign countenances. Outwardly, they appear to have no woes, but our parents have told us their story of immense suffering endured in Europe when the Nazis suddenly arrested several family members.

The Zetzas were spared because they were out walking at the time. Despite repeated efforts, they were unable to find information regarding the fate of their loved ones. When they were offered passage on a steamer to Shanghai, they left all their worldly possessions behind, and fled the holocaust on one of the last steamers allowed to leave the shores of Europe. Anyone who had heard about the Chinese safe haven with no visa requirements had scrambled to buy tickets on these old ships, hoping permission to leave would not be denied, as was often the case.

Mrs. Zetza seats us and immediately ladles huge portions of oily noodles into three large white bowls, encouraging us to consume the entire nauseating, slippery mound. Gagging, I wonder whether our mother had sanctioned this excessive punishment that we still recall with horror. (It occurs to me now that the Zetzas never ate noodles with us). Now and then, Mr. Zetza rubs his hand over his practically bald head where some small patches of white hair randomly sprout on his shiny pate. He has taught me a song that is really very sad. It goes like this:

*Goodbye Mom, Goodbye Pop, Goodbye Mule with the great big horns.*
*I don't know, what the war is about, but I bet by God I'll soon find out.*
*Goodbye Dearie, don't you fear. I'll bring you back a souvenir.*
*I'll bring you a Turk and the Kaiser too, and that's about all that I can do.*

Mr. Zetza's eyes glisten and I wonder whether I see tears. He sings in a low croaky voice and I join in with gusto. I love music, and from an early age had already shown signs of musical talent. Many members of our family were musically gifted.

# FLOODS IN THE INTERNATIONAL SETTLEMENT

The rains came early in June, once again flooding the surrounding areas and streets of the International Settlement. The typhoon, which means big wind, blew with a fury that shattered windows and brought down huge tree branches, injuring many and creating havoc. Some claimed that the Chinese, knowing this particular area was regularly flooded, had conceded it to us after the British won the opium wars. Our road had really bad drainage, and was always one of the worst areas during the rainy season. Brown, muddy water ran down the streets, collecting all the bits of garbage it could find along the way, bringing with it the promise of more death from cholera, malaria and other diseases.

Bare-footed rickshaw pullers, wearing skimpy rainproof capes, were running themselves ragged, to milk out as many fares as possible while the rain held. In some places the water was two feet deep. Each footfall sent great splashes in all directions, and loud cursing and shouting was heard every now and then as someone fell and was drenched. Passengers in rickshaws and pedicabs were seated behind waterproof screens, barely able to see where they were being taken in these chaotic conditions, but happy to be part of the privileged society. Here and there, cars had stalled when their engines flooded.

We wore knee-high galoshes that covered and protected our shoes from the deep, dirty water, where we would have sloshed about happily all day, if allowed. Gradually, as we outgrew these rubber boots, finally wearing them with only our socks underneath, they were handed down the line to younger family members. Enjoying ourselves, we were oblivious to danger as we watched an occasional dead rodent, cat, or other small animal float by, part of the debris which would finally end up in the creek. These animals were probably already dead when they were washed up from some drain or other hidden spots in the area.

Amah was always nearby, keeping a watchful eye on us. She sat on a stool or stood in any convenient shelter, where she chatted and gossiped loudly with anyone sharing the space. Now and then she scolded us loudly, "David, why you touch that dirty thing. Leave alone. We go home if you no listen. Too much washing when you so dirty." The truth is, she enjoyed being out of the apartment, away from household chores.

Amah diligently hangs on to her colorful, hand-painted, oilpaper umbrella, guarding it from theft by lurking, nimble street urchins, waiting for an opportunity to rob absent-minded victims! It has colorful, hand-painted birds and flowers on it, and a bamboo handle. The Chinese are widely believed to have invented umbrellas—at least two thousand years ago. They were first made of silk. Later, they waxed and lacquered paper parasols, rendering them water-repellant. The finished product went through multiple processes before emerging as a durable, pretty umbrella. In ancient times, royal families used red and yellow umbrellas, and common people only used blue ones.

My own smaller, colorful waxed umbrella was pink. We had a few at home—they were very cheap, and available in all sizes and colors at nearby Seymour Road market and many other shopping places.

Sometimes, when the rains came early and the flooding was really unmanageable, schools closed ahead of schedule for the June summer holidays. The kids loved that situation, even though, eventually, the last weeks of the break seemed interminable. Everyone was bored and edgy, and parents had run out of innovative ideas.

Often, we visited my maternal grandparents who shared the big three-storey house with some of their adult and married children. Although they lived in China for many decades, they never mastered the English language and had an extremely limited vocabulary, so it was hard to communicate in depth. A few words, accompanied by smiles and hugs, seemed to cover all basic, essential communication. Love was the cement that bonded us.

Granny always welcomed us with open arms and kisses. "How are you, Darling? You want to eat something?" Her pantry shelves were full of delicious pre-cooked food and multicolored, homemade pickled vegetables in glass jars. She was a wonderful cook. In no time, we were being fed special delicacies from a seemingly endless supply of Sephardic-style cooked chicken, rice, meat dishes and pastries that she offered her happily accepting grandchildren.

Sometimes I watched Granny skillfully "undress" a raw chicken! She, my mother and her sisters, were able to remove the entire skin in one piece, and stuff it with raw rice, herbs and other ingredients. They sewed both ends closed, and boiled it. The rice swelled, until the skin looked exactly like a whole intact chicken. Then they browned the skin until it crackled. It was sliced, served, attractive and delicious!

Another favorite recipe was *Hamim*, prepared on Friday, and slow-cooked overnight in observance of the law prohibiting cooking on the Sabbath. Many variations exist, but our recipe usually included rice, beef or chicken, carrots, and semolina dumplings.

The house was always full of people and activity. Mummy's brothers, Isaac, Jack, and their extended families lived there, as well as her younger unwed brothers, Moses and David.

Although old, long-standing prejudices regarding marriages between Sephardim and Ashkenazim were fading, Granny was not entirely charmed with Isaac and Jack's choice of Polish and Russian wives. I suspect her inability to communicate with them in English led to misunderstandings, and compounded the problem.

*We* liked them very much. Mummy had introduced her friend Riva to Jack, who married her.

When he was not working, Grandpa spent most of his leisure time in prayer. Although he seldom spoke with us, we felt how much he loved us all and how welcome we were in his home.

# HONGKEW

Many European Jews had already arrived in Shanghai during the years preceding the infamous Kristalnacht, in November, 1938. Also referred to as Crystal Night, the Night of Broken Glass, it marked a series of coordinated attacks against Jews throughout Nazi Germany which left streets covered with glass from smashed windows of Jewish-owned property and synagogues. Homes, hospitals, and schools were ransacked, buildings demolished with sledgehammers, over 7,000 businesses were destroyed or damaged, and over 1,000 synagogues burned.

The early immigrants to Shanghai had come with money and were established and doing quite well. Generally well educated, they contributed a great deal to the cultural and educational development of the community. Those forced to flee after Kristalnacht were less fortunate, and found themselves in an extremely sad plight.

The Sephardim and Russian Jews helped the new arrivals generously with accommodation, soup kitchens, supplies and financial assistance.

The European newcomers faced a multitude of obstacles. They were unprepared for the indigenous diseases and unsanitary conditions. Their clothing was unsuitable for the extreme climatic variables, from freezing winters to hot humid summers and a rainy season that regularly flooded Shanghai's roadways. Not least of their problems was the linguistic barrier. Very few had a working knowledge of English, which, despite their skills and education levels, was a tremendous handicap when seeking employment in

Shanghai's business world.

No license was required to practice a profession or operate a business, which was an advantage—particularly for doctors. A number of naive, unwary refugees, believing false promises of wealth through business deals and partnerships, were swindled out of all their money by Shanghai's unscrupulous, professional crooks.

The refugees eventually numbered between seventeen and eighteen thousand, imposing a strain on the already heavily populated city's resources. In August 1939, the Japanese finally succumbed to mounting pressure from influential Shanghai groups to stem the massive influx. They closed the gates. And *most* countries of the world, doing very little to aid, sealed entries and denied visas to Jewish refugees.

Eventually, the burden of providing shelter and aid became too difficult and complicated to be handled solely by the Committee for the Assistance of European Jewish Refugees in Shanghai. Several additional committees were formed to deal with finance, housing, medical care, educational and cultural aspects, employment and rehabilitation. Everything was run efficiently and new departments were added as the need arose.

Despite being allied with Germany, the Japanese never adopted the fascist ideology. Even when Germany sent Colonel Meissinger to Shanghai with special orders, the Japanese refused their suggested plans to carry out a "final solution." They never forgot, and were grateful that in 1904, when everyone else refused aid, a Jewish American banker, Jacob Schiff, had helped finance their war against Russia. Other wealthy Sephardim had also loaned them large sums of money in past years, which led the Japanese to believe all Jews were wealthy, and wielded power. Another speculated theory is that they wanted a bargaining chip with the Americans if they lost the war.

For the most part, the Japanese left the Jews alone and allowed them to pass freely through the city.

Nevertheless, the Nazi regime imposed their will on the Japanese, who complied with a decree that all stateless refugees who had arrived in Shanghai since 1937 were to be incarcerated in a designated restricted area.

On February 18, 1943, a notice was posted that read:

# PROCLAMATION
## CONCERNING RESTRICTION OF RESIDENCE AND BUSINESS OF STATELESS REFUGEES

(1)  Due to military necessity, places of residence and business of the stateless refugees in the Shanghai area shall hereafter be restricted to the under mentioned area in the International Settlement. East of the line connecting Chaofoong Road, Muirhead Road and Dent Road; West of Yangtsepoo Creek; North of the line connecting East Seward Road and Wayside Road; and South of the boundary of the International Settlement.

(2)  The Stateless refugees at present residing and/or carrying on business in the districts other than the above area shall remove their places of residence and/or business into the area designated above by May 18, 1943. Permission must be obtained from the Japanese authorities for the transfer, sale, purchase or lease of room, houses, shops or any other establishments which are situated outside the Designated Area and are now being used by the Stateless refugees.

(3) Persons other than the Stateless refugees shall not remove into the area mentioned in Article (1) without permission of the Japanese authorities.

(4) Persons who will have violated this Proclamation or obstructed its enforcement shall be liable to severe punishment.

Commander-in-Chief of the Imperial Japanese Army in the Shanghai Area.

The Japanese Proclamation never used the word "Jews."


The stateless refugees from Germany, Austria or Poland, stripped of documents and forced to leave Europe empty-handed, all fell into this category. They had no choice but to comply with the edict, exchanging their well-tended homes for shabby, squalid Japanese dwellings in the foul-smelling slums of Hongkew, also known since 1937 as "Little Tokyo," and later as Yangtsepoo. For many years it was dominated by a strong Japanese influence.

Less than one square mile in size, the overcrowded, dilapidated, grimy-walled, rat-infested ghetto already housed an estimated 100,000 Chinese living in abject squalor. Refugees living in Hongkew at the time numbered about 8,000. With the implementation of the ghetto proclamation, this figure more or less doubled. They shared the area with these ancient people who suffered tremendously from the war. The Japanese had killed and wounded more than thirty million Chinese civilians and soldiers, plundered and burnt villages and cities, raped countless women and reduced vast areas to rubble.

In spite of their own wretched, miserable plight, the Chinese were kind and generous to the refugees, treating them with empathy, warmth, and friendliness. Chinese and Jewish children played games together in the narrow streets and alleys, where hungry dogs chased mangy cats that fed on a bounty of over-sized rats. The children learnt a smattering of each other's language—enough to carry on *game-business* as usual, and exchange niceties or swear words!

The appalling, cramped living conditions, lack of sanitation, and inadequate medical attention and supplies led to devastating illnesses. Clean drinking water and nourishing food were in short supply, causing large-scale malnutrition. About fifteen hundred refugees died from various causes during their incarceration.

It was not an unusual sight to see corpses of straw-bundled Chinese babies and emaciated, disease-stricken adults lying in doorways of alleys and streets, before being collected by The Chinese Benevolent Society.

Notwithstanding their acute poverty, suffering and hardship, the refugees were determined to keep up their cultural activities, and somehow managed to organize artistic, literary, and educational programs. They produced theatrical productions, musical events, and printed newspapers.

Ghoya, the Japanese Commandant of Hongkew, pronounced himself "King of the Jews." He was a short, evil-tempered man, who used to stand on a table, glowering, yelling, jumping, and pounding anything or anyone at hand. Paradoxically, he also played the violin and sometimes recruited refugee musicians to perform with him.

If they found a job, the refugees were issued arbitrary temporary passes to work outside the incarceration area. But often, on a whim, Ghoya would sadistically keep them waiting long hours in a line, or deny daily passes. He slapped faces for no apparent reason, and reveled in complete control and power.

Many Jews, still living freely outside the various incarceration areas, created fictitious jobs to help refugees receive exit passes. Permission, granted at the discretion of Ghoya and the Japanese authorities, was often denied.

After the first year, the permits were drastically curtailed.

Infringements were severely dealt with. One of many signs displayed on plaques along the ghetto's boundaries read:

## STATELESS REFUGEES
### ARE **PROHIBITED** TO PASS
### HERE WITHOUT PERMISSION

On July 17, 1945, in one of a growing number of U.S. air raids on Shanghai, twenty-five Douglas twin A-26 bombers took off from Okinawa carrying 100-pound bombs. Amongst their intended targets was a Japanese radio transmitter in the Hongkew district, and the Chiangwan airfield.

Horrifically, some of the bombs fell on the Hongkew ghetto. The devastating strikes killed two-hundred-and-fifty people—thirty-one of them refugees—wounded five hundred and left several hundred homeless.

In spite of these miserable conditions, the broad opinion was their fate was better than that of loved-ones and friends left behind to be murdered in the German extermination camps and the rest of Europe.

Chiune Sugihara, the Japanese Ambassador in Lithuania, was noted among those who saved many refugees. Until the day of his departure from Europe, he defied orders from superiors to stop, and issued thousands of visas to Kobe, Japan, providing the recipients showed they intended to progress to another destination. One obvious choice was Shanghai, a port with no visa requirement. The average stay in Japan was eight months, or longer for some. The Japanese, not usually partial to foreigners living in their country, permitted them to stay and treated them well. Generous inhabitants of Kobe gave or shared their food rations with the Jews, and some doctors administered free medical treatment and inoculations. Israel posthumously honored Sugihara, and awarded him the title of "Righteous Gentile."

Feng-Shan Ho, Chinese consul-general in Vienna during 1938-1940, also disobeyed orders to desist, and issued thousands of visas to Shanghai to all requesting them—including those leaving Nazi Germany for other destinations. The Commission for the Designation of the Righteous awarded him the title of "Righteous Among the Nations."

In April 1994, the following commemorative plaque, in Chinese, English and Hebrew, was dedicated by the Hongkew district government:

## THE DESIGNATED AREA FOR STATELESS REFUGEES

From 1937 to 1941, thousands of Jews came to Shanghai fleeing from Nazi persecution. Japanese occupation authorities regarded them as "stateless refugees" and set up this designated area to restrict their residence and business. The designated area was bordered on the west by Gongping Road, on the east by Tongbei Road, on the south by Huiming Road, and on the north by Zhoujiazui Road.

Hongkou District People's Government.

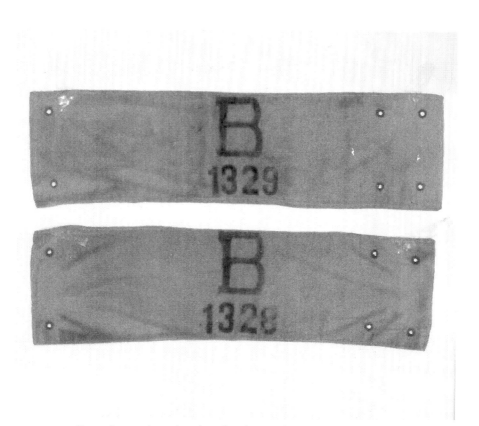

Compulsory red numbered armbands worn by Benjy and Liza Benjamin.

# THE JAPANESE OCCUPATION

The day after Pearl Harbor was bombed, on December 7, 1941, the ubiquitous Japanese wasted no time occupying and controlling Shanghai. Their original insidious infiltration into China was now an earnest, relentless take-over. They speedily began sealing off all the city's business and office safes, severely limiting and eliminating accessibility to files and personal effects.

My father said, "We knew, right away, that we had to obey all orders put out by the Japanese."

They went into Daddy's office and demanded to know, "Who's in charge of this office? What is the office business? What is so-and-so?"

"Warehouse," my father answered.

"Whose is this? Come on. Where are the keys—let's go to your warehouses. Put the keys on the top," they instructed officiously, pointing to an office cabinet.

Incredibly, my father had managed to remove all the money from the safe of one of his warehouses before they arrived. Then he told my mother he couldn't bring another penny home because the Japanese sealed the other warehouse safe. "But," he told her, "my money was in the bank and I got it all out!"

"But you had some money in the safe. And the banks were also sealed," my mother reminded him.

"Yes—but I took it all—I had my money! The banks were closed, but when they opened again, people could go and take money in and out, to live. So—all that time I only had about $15,000 in the bank. I didn't know if my money was there or not. The Japanese said, 'We will give you *so much*, naming an amount, so you can pay all your people back.' So I got my money back, because I took it all out of the bank and put it in the safe—and then I could live off it. But when the time came the Japanese took the business over and then *they* paid all the salaries…

"I took my personal files away—because they didn't watch every man going out every one or two hours, carrying things. But, big books and all that—you couldn't take ledgers, journals, and cashbooks, in or out, without the Japanese supervisor knowing.

"The Chinese came and said, 'I want my cargo.' They wanted their shirts, materials—whatever they had in our warehouses. The Japanese office supervisor saw that we gave him the warrant to go and get all his things. It was not ours," my father emphasized. "It was the people's cargo—general public's cargo.

"Until a month or two later, we weren't allowed to go to the office any more. Finished—because they took over! They did the same with all big British and American firms. The Japanese were now master of all business in Shanghai. Oil Company, Tramways, Bus and Gas Company, and private industry—all, all… everything like that. They took every damn thing! But they didn't kick you out—like, *get out tomorrow and don't come back*! Slowly, they got you out… then they just left important, key men with the companies, until they learnt how to take over and run everything on their own."

My father had about five hundred merchants with cargo in the warehouses, and issued warrants for release of any merchandise. Anyone who wanted his cargo had to show a bill of lading as proof of ownership. If he owed the bank money he had to receive a verification stamp on the warrant stating, "This man has paid us," before he was permitted to remove his goods.

Newspapers and radios advised everyone to be ready, and announced:

*British residents who need any advice, assistance, or anything else, should go to the British Residents Association (BRA) in such-and-such a place, in Cathedral Church.*

Americans and Belgians also had their own place to go to for help.

"From January to March, April, and May, people began to feel the blow," my father said. "They started lining up. It was going slowly at first, but then it suddenly became very hard...

"They helped those who were destitute. People like us couldn't go and take money, because we didn't need it right away. We managed until summertime—six or eight months—when we started to need. Then we had to say, 'Where can we get money from? How do we live?'"

"And afterwards, we went," my mother said, entering the conversation. "Every month The BRA were giving us a sack full of cracked wheat, with a recipe how to make bread. We had enough—we had a lot. A whole sack a month! And I baked several loaves, and was even able to help people who didn't have any."

"But then we had to pay for it." My father stated.

"They helped us—we had to pay very little, *very* little, always. I remember it, Benjy, because *I* baked. I still have the recipe."

"*You* baked, but I was the one who had to go and bring it in. I stood in line every month, paid for it, and took it. Liza—I'm not in the mood for all this!"

I didn't know whether to be amused or vexed by this little conflict that arose between my parents. I realized they always enjoyed this type of argument—at times it seemed almost to be a family trait! Anxious to continue, I managed, albeit with difficulty, to get them back on track.

"We made a monthly statement," my father continued, "saying, 'please, I need so much a month...' If you were on the list, you got money once a month from the BRA cashier. Then, if you needed cracked wheat or something, you went to get it from them. 'Please, I need 5lbs, 3lbs...' You paid maybe one-tenth, or one-fifteenth, of the price outside. If they gave you the wheat you wanted—for five persons in the family—you got it and paid cash, because you had money from the cashier in your pocket."

"And they kept on helping all through, until we were interned," my mother said, having the last word on the subject.

Despite a persistent sense of foreboding, and the inescapable, ominous, pervasive presence of the occupiers, everyday life appeared, outwardly at least, to carry on with a semblance of normalcy. Everyone was told when and where to receive compulsory red armbands with black identifying letters and numbers.

The Chinese were forced to bow, scrape, and don their hats to the Japanese, and whether they complied or not, often suffered blows, serious abuse, and bodily injury. But, notwithstanding the magnitude of their own difficulties, they exhibited smug satisfaction at the plight of the "reduced" foreigners, reveling in their perceived "loss of face."

Mummy said, "We carried on exactly as we had before—always. I still went to the YMCA and met up with my friend Tulita, who would be going to Ash camp, and several others—all of us would soon be interned in various camps, on different entry dates."

# DADDY GIVES UP HIS CAR

*It's March 1941—Purim day, a joyful Jewish holiday. We usually dress in carnival clothes, entertain, and have fun. As told in the scroll of the story of Esther—my own name—it remembers our victory over oppression.*

*But I'm not even dressing up as the queen—no one is happy today…*

Daddy came home from the Japanese compound. He was wearing his degrading red armband. The number "1328" is printed beneath the prominent, bold, black "B." To the occupying powers Daddy is just another number—1328, and Mummy is number 1329.

All allies of Britain and America were notified that on certain specified dates they were to deliver their cars to the Japanese at a designated compound.

"I don't think I'll ever see my car again," he told Mummy dejectedly. "They said 'put it on the scale,' and then they gave me this Japanese 'toilet paper,' with a signature and a lot of rubbish on it, that says, 'we got a car.'" He showed Mummy the paper. "Then they ordered me to get out!"

Daddy was so proud of his shiny black Packard. He was one of a growing group of privileged motorcar owners since December 1904, when the first car landed in Shanghai. Sometimes it broke down and had to be cranked and pushed, but we didn't mind because we loved it so much. Now we would all have to use trams, pedicabs, and rickshaws again. We didn't always travel by car because Daddy used it for business, but on weekends we took wonderful rides that I was surely going to miss. I felt like crying.

Some of Daddy's friends and acquaintances delivered their cars the same day. "Everyone was miserable—some had tears in their eyes," he told Mummy, in a strange, cracking kind of voice.

"Don't worry. We'll have fun anyway, and soon we'll get the car back." Mummy tried to reassure us. She was always optimistic and strong, and led us the same way she led her girl guides of the Ninth Shanghai Jewish Company, at their weekly meetings. They took it all very seriously— helping people whenever possible, and performing a good deed every day. We all joined in whenever she sang their song at home:

> We're the girl guides marching on the King's highway
> With a step that's light and a heart that's gay
> And there's room for me, and there's room for you
> And there's work in the world for the guides to do.
> As the stars that shine overhead to cheer
> We try to learn how to shine down here.
> Lend a hand, comrade mine,
> Lend a hand, lend a hand.

Very soon we were going into camp. I wasn't sure what that meant, but our family, some of our relatives and friends, were spending hours making lists and shopping for funny things like camp beds, and tin cups and dishes. Mummy was also buying canned foods and kosher salami that could hang in the air and stay fresh for a long time. "We'll be going on a picnic," she told us. Sometimes she would pretend going into camp was fun—singing a lilting refrain—We're going into camp, we're going into camp.

But I heard the adults saying glumly that this was a difficult war, and they hoped it wouldn't last too long.

Many years later, I asked my parents, "How did you know you must take rations to camp? Who told you?"

My father said, "When they knew they were calling people in, one told the other—'prepare yourselves, take things, and take rain shoes. Take food that you think can last for a while.' They spoke among themselves— bachelors and wives who were left out. Husbands went in together, and one told the other, 'take this, take that.' So we used most of the money we got for a month's expenses and took lots of stuff in with us."

"Were you in a very, very bad state when you had to go to the camp? Were you upset, crying and all that?" Although I had my own childish memories I could not possibly, at age five, have had total perception and comprehension of our plight.

"Of course we were not happy, but we had to make the best of the situation," my father said, with resignation. "You know, after all, being British you had to act British…"

"Yes—stiff upper lip!" *How ridiculous*, I thought to myself. "And so, you took rations and other things. Did they last for a short, short time?"

"No, no! They lasted a long time," my father answered. "We went in Pessach 1943, and it lasted until almost end of the year. We took every damn thing! Many people had nothing—they went in with nothing, and were in a worse condition. Not everybody had somebody to advise them."

Daddy called in some Chinese carpenters, who made a lot of noise and created piles of sawdust while cutting up our wardrobes and other wooden furniture. I watched them work speedily and very skillfully. Pretty soon the pieces were nailed and glued together to emerge as functional trunks to hold our belongings in camp. Although my parents tried to show a brave face, I knew they were very distressed to see their lovely furniture hacked to pieces, and to face the uncertainty of their future as POWs.

Mummy took down our floral chintz curtains. The extra, unused fabric seat covers for the car were brought from the closet. She measured us, made some paper patterns and carefully cut the material. Her Singer sewing machine whirred loudly as she stitched long seams. Pretty soon, the girls in our family had new, colorful overalls to wear in camp.

There were a lot of loud bangs from bombs and shooting going on constantly. I could see the adults were shocked and frightened. They never thought Shanghai would have any real problem, and felt the International Settlement would be immune from any Japanese attack.

Until December 8, 1941, when the Japanese ship, *Idzumo*, sank the British gunboat, *HMS Peterel*, the atrocities had mainly focused on the Chinese. The *Peterel* was attacked after it refused demands to surrender. Now we were considered enemies of Japan, who had joined Germany against the Allies.

The Japanese were ripping out steel fences, confiscating radiators, machinery, and anything that could be melted down and recycled for the war effort.

My parents, and many others destined for internment, listened with distress to English-language, anti-Allied radio broadcasts from Berlin that frequently taunted Allied forces. The hateful Nazi broadcasting-propagandist with the smarmy nasal drawl was American-born William Joyce, nicknamed "Lord Haw-Haw."

Joyce had lived in England since infancy, but fled to Germany in 1939 and joined the Nazi Party. Deeply anti-Semitic, he blamed "Jewish Communists" for most of the era's social and political ills, and never disguised his admiration for Hitler and Nazi policies.

Although laughed at and denounced by many, including journalists—who regarded the obviously propagandistic content as absurd, and dismissed him as a stooge—listeners were occasionally frightened by the accurate, descriptive details of British towns and landmarks. Nevertheless, hopeful of gleaning information about loved ones on the battlefront, they listened to the infuriating, exaggerated reports of inflated losses and casualties of Allied forces, and the shooting down and sinking of Allied aircraft and ships.

These details were frequently the only ones available concerning the fate of those missing after bombing missions over Germany.

At the end of the war the infamous and hated William Joyce, alias "Lord Haw-Haw," was captured in Germany after being shot in the leg while trying to escape into a wood. He was flown back to Britain, convicted of treason, sentenced to death by gallows, and executed in 1946.

# THE NOTICE

Early in 1943, the following dreaded notice finally arrived. We had anticipated its arrival for a long time—ever since the first notices were sent out over a year ago. We escaped earlier internment because the Japanese were insufficiently organized or equipped to cope with a huge, simultaneous influx.

My parents had been wearing red armbands since January1941, when the incarceration decree was issued—before the first intake occurred. Despite knowledge of their impending imprisonment, they stared at the notice with dismay and disbelief, and read the instructions, replete with grammatical errors, that would shortly change their lives forever.

## NOTICE

To Mr. B. F. BENJAMIN

By military necessity, you and your family are hereby ordered to live in the Civil Assembly Centre. Necessary preparations shall accordingly be made by you as follows:

(1)  To be present at the Public and Thomas Hanbury School for Boys, 404 Yu Yuen Road, by 10 a.m., April 21st, 1943

(2)  Your entrance numbers are: Entrance No.

(a) Head of family:    Mr. B. F. BENJAMIN    ................
(b) Wife:              Mrs. L. M. BENJAMIN...................
(c) Children:Name:     D.H.R. BENJAMIN       ................
                       E.R. BENJAMIN         ................
                       S.P. BENJAMIN         ................

(111)Your properties shall be disposed of according to the following:

(A)  The commodities and others itemized hereunder are to be brought to
     the Civil Assembly Centre.

   (a) Things of daily use, personal effects, cash, valuable papers,
       passport and other personal papers, etc. shall be packed up in
       small portable suitcases, etc. which each person can easily carry
       and be conveyed by yourself on the day of assembly.

   (b) Others:

      (1) Beddings; bedstead; mattress; sheets; blankets; quilts; and
          mosquito-nets adjustable to the bed.

      (2) Clothings:

          For each person one or two suits for spring, summer,
          autumn, and winter wear; underwear; two or three pairs of
          shoe; four or five pairs of slippers.

      (3) Table wares:

          For each person four or five dishes; cups; spoons; a vacuum-
          bottle; knives and forks; napkins and table-cloths.

      (4) Goods for sports and amusement; books and stocked
          provisions, if desired.

      (5) Note:

      (a) The things mentioned above must be simple and unostentatious,
          strong and durable.

      (b) The goods itemized above shall be packed up and labeled with
          the owner's name, nationality, and the number of entrance
          with the Civil Assembly Centre and shall be sent to the Public
          & Thomas Hanbury School for Boys, 404 Yu Yuen Road, one
          day previous to day of entrance.

      (c) The office for receiving the above will be open from 10 a.m. to

3 p.m. on March 24th, 1943.

(d) As no responsibility will be taken by the Japanese authorities for the damage which might be incurred during the transportation, careful packing is advised.

(e) The number of packages of goods permitted shall not exceed
............

(B)  With the exception of those items mentioned under (A), the specified furnitures and fixtures such as desks, chairs, tables, bedsteads, mattresses, bathtubs, electric wires and illuminators, wardrobes, cupboards, telephones, refrigerators, electric fans, stoves, cooking stoves, carpets, radio-sets and curtains which fall within the purview of Article III of the Proclamation issued on November 13th, 1942 in the names of the Commanders-in-Chief of the Japanese Army and Navy in the Shanghai area, shall be left in the house as they are.

(C)  The goods or merchandise which have been prohibited to remove, to sell or to dispose by the previous Proclamations issued by the Commander-in-Chief of the Japanese Army and Navy shall also be left in the present locality.

(D)  Silverwares, jewels and souvenirs may be packed in cases and entrusted with the Protective Power. The said cases shall be left unnailed with the respective Consulates-General in charge of enemy interest for the inspection of the Japanese authorities.

(E)  The other articles not included in (A), (B) and (C) may be sold or disposed of at your discretion. The money realized by such disposals can be taken to the Civil Assembly Centre. As to the articles not disposed of before the time of assembly, they shall be either left in your home or shall be entrusted with G. E. Marden & Co.'s No. 15 Godown, Race Course Market, packed and labeled with your name and entrance number together with a detailed list thereof. Articles left or entrusted shall be disposed of by the Japanese authorities on your behalf.

(F)  On leaving for the Civil Assembly Centre, you shall lock and seal your dwelling securely, and for the time being you may place your dwelling under the administration of your friend or relative (until it shall be administered by the Japanese authorities). In case of an apartment or boarding house your rooms shall be taken care of by the administrator thereof.

(1V)   On the day of your removal, you shall wear on your left breast a card showing your entrance number and shall bring and submit to the Japanese officials at the Public & Thomas Hanbury School for Boys and envelope (attached herewith) enclosing
  (a) Keys of your dwelling and of properties left behind,
  (b) Two copies of the plan showing the location and dwelling,
  (c) List of articles left behind in triplicate,
  (d) List of articles brought to the Civil Assembly Centre in duplicate,
  (e) A statement giving the name and address of the administrator of your dwelling, if appointed.

  NOTE: (Your name and entrance number should be clearly written on the envelope)

(V)   In case you have any question concerning this notice, you should make enquiries with the Japanese Consulate-General and act in accordance with their instructions.

Signed:
Consul-General for Japan.

## CAKES AND TEARS

A few days before we went into camp, Mummy wore a pretty hat and gloves and took us on a tram to the Bund. The crowded tram clanged, and made a lot of noise, but we didn't mind because it was an adventure. I loved to look out the window and watch rickshaws, bicycles, and other vehicles going past. There was always so much to see on the way to the exciting waterfront; huge creative buildings, sideshows, fortune-tellers, performing monkeys, Chinese scribes, and an occasional funeral procession. The tantalizing aroma of roasting chestnuts, peanuts, sunflower seeds, and sweet potatoes, corn on the cob boiling in huge barrels, rice cakes and other delicacies— all offered by street vendors—permeated the air.

Finally arriving, we saw huge ships, and hundreds of junks sailing up and down. The pulsating sounds of life on the water were, as always, both deafening and exciting. The area thronged with people from every walk of life.

"We're going to meet Auntie Prissy," Mummy announced, "and we'll have tea and cream cakes at *Chaklianne's*." What a treat awaited us. *Chaklianne's* was a wonderful Russian coffee shop and bakery on the Bund. I couldn't understand why Mummy and Auntie Prissy were so tearful; whispering kind words and reassuring each other they would meet again very soon. She was Mummy's best friend, and both were petite and pretty. They were competitive sportspeople, who played volleyball and other games together at the foreign YMCA, on Bubbling Well Road.

Auntie Prissy wasn't going into camp because she was Portuguese and not considered an enemy of Japan.

On the way home Mummy hardly spoke to us, seemingly lost in her own sad thoughts. She never smiled once and didn't pay attention when David and I argued. After a while we also became subdued, because it seemed half the fun of arguing was taken away when we couldn't get Mummy's attention.

My parents spent hours pondering over what to do with all our valuable things. At first they sold a whole lot to a junk dealer, and got some cash to buy food and other essentials. Then Mr. Yip, Daddy's employee, came over and collected the remainder of our silver and valuables for safekeeping during our internment. "Mr. Ben-jee," he said reassuringly, "don't worry about these things. I promise I look after them for you. Soon you come back and everything will be OK again, like before." He shook his head in a kind of sad disbelief, and stroked some of our beautiful ornaments while he put them together with the silver cutlery into two large cane suitcases, that looked just like my little one that I loved.

We had no choice but to trust Mr. Yip. He had worked for several years as Daddy's *Comprador*—an important man who oversaw the smooth running of business, and acted as a go-between for the foreigners and the Chinese. Many Compradors became very wealthy in Shanghai, where it was common for squeeze money to be paid for business "favours." This form of bribery, acknowledged and accepted as a fact of life, would often benefit several people in a business chain.

On the first evening of *Pessach*, (Passover) in April 1943, we tearfully celebrated the *Seder*, eating matzoth and performing all the rituals. This was to be our last wonderful home-cooked festival meal for a long time.

The next morning Mummy and Daddy looked around our home for the last time. In a crying mood, we all said "goodbye" to our weeping Amah. Sylvia was howling and clinging to her beloved Amah, whom she didn't want to leave. She was inconsolable and had to be torn away.

Some Chinese men with large wheelbarrows arrived to collect our things. They grunted and chanted while they delivered all our cases, kitbags, beds, and bare necessities to the Public Boys and Girls school on Yu Yuen Road, our designated camp, and "home" for the unforeseeable future.

Our apartment on Nan Yang Road was not a great distance from Yu Yuen Road, so we walked with them. They dumped everything unceremoniously in a heap at the front gates, where they lay together with the tangled up possessions of other internees arriving the same day. Several of them were our friends and acquaintances. Some had delivered their possessions to the gates several days before their own arrival and were now searching frantically for their goods. People were shouting and crying.

Chaos reigned.

Smug, faintly sneering Japanese guards stood at the entrance, waiting for us to enter the enclosure. There was no way out of it. With resignation and a great deal of dignity, we passed through the gates, from freedom to captivity.

# FROM FREEDOM TO CAPTIVITY

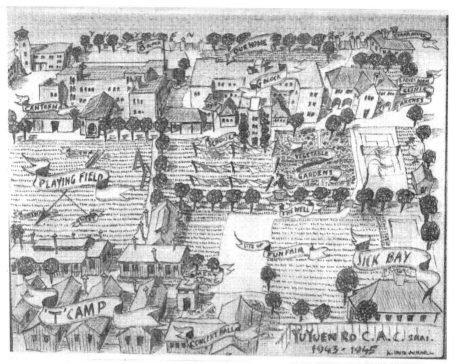

Artist's hand-drawn map of Yu Yuen Road camp. John Kenneth Smith-Mitchell was Art Editor of Camp ChitChat, YuYuen Road Camp "newspaper".

Entrance to Yu Yuen Road Camp. Previously Shanghai Public School for girls.

# CAPTIVES

A small batch of hollow-eyed, underfed internees watched sadly as a welcoming group led us to our designated building and family room, in the Public Girls School. They were the earlier arrivals, some of whom had already been interned for a year. Friends and acquaintances were amongst them, and they greeted us warmly. The Japanese, unprepared for such an overwhelming intake, had staggered incarceration dates…

In 1986 I visited my parents in Israel. At the time I was living in South Africa. My father was convalescing after a serious bout of pneumonia, and I was driven by the urgency of his illness to get any information I could before we ran out of time.

I armed myself with a tape recorder and began a series of several extensive interviews of both parents, beginning with that visit, and ending with a final tape of my mother in 2004. My father passed away in 2002.

Many years before, my attempts to record our story were aborted because my father, finding it too painful, stubbornly refused to be reminded of his life in Shanghai. He resisted any discussion related to family difficulties, or internment. I was aware that, because of my youth at the time, there were many gaps in my knowledge and perception of events during the war years.

Being consistently thwarted only sharpened my burning desire to record our experiences in detail. I mulled over everything I already knew and remembered. That just raised more questions, jogged my memory, and caused me an indefinable pain. Sometimes I had moments of sudden insight—into my parents' and our family's emotions during that period.

I was struck by my father's willingness, even eagerness, finally, to share his painful memories. His acceptance of everything that happened, without real complaint, astonished me. He attributed it to his deep religious faith and regular prayers. "That's what saved me," he said. "You don't know, Ester," he sighed, "you just don't know…"

It was relatively easy to get information from my mother, and sometimes, when he said "enough," I turned to *her* with questions, only to have my father say, "No Liza! No—it was not like that!" And he would continue answering again.

In 2001, at age ninety-one, his voice had faded considerably and despite his understandable memory lapses, I was able to tape a huge additional amount of information.

"How did you feel during those early days of internment?" I asked my mother.

"We were lucky to be among the later arrivals," she said, "because we were with very small children, and they were taking our lot last, so we went in quite a few months after the others. And that's why we sort of knew we had to take more foodstuff. When we went in—with practically nothing—people were so hungry. We felt very sorry for them.

"Our particular camp was comprised of families as well as single people," she told me. "It was mainly for people in official positions and high office, like people from the police force. Although some *were* interned together, many husbands were taken in earlier, right away, and their wives later. Even the Commissioner of Police was there. He was head of the whole camp.

"There were two dormitories for singles—one each for women and men, because many husbands and wives were separated, and incarcerated elsewhere."

"How many people were in each dormitory?" I asked.

"A lot! A hundred—or over a hundred. And of course, there were lots of affairs, and some marriages were practically broken up. You'd be surprised at how much was going on!"

"A hundred people in a dormitory—in one long room? Were the

beds very close to each other?"

"Not particularly, but not *so* far," Mummy said. "It was a very big room—there were a lot of people. Remember the halls we had at my former school? That's what they used. Young women, old women, and even young girls who couldn't live with their parents in a little room—were also in the dormitory."

"Did they get on with each other, all those people?"

"The women were so busy—each had her own business to do. There were all sorts of little troubles and they had minor squabbles, but the place was very organized, because mostly officials were there first.

"Two men from the dormitories escaped one night, and the Japanese punished everybody," she said.

"How did they escape?" I asked my father. "Were there any tunnel attempts?"

"They crawled through," he said, "under the barbed wire."

"And—did you know about any secret radio transmitters?"

"That meant certain death if any man had a radio or something!" he said. "There were one or two people who had some small things—but nobody knew about it. We only know they never transmitted *outside*— they only received…"


Soon it became evident the Japanese were determined to show us who was in control. We had morning and evening roll calls, standing in rows in the assembly hall. "Three or four guards marched in, one carrying a stick. They paraded sternly up and down, slapping a face now and then," Mummy said. "One used to take the roll call—number one, two, three… We all had numbers. We couldn't leave the hall until they had finished inspecting our quarters and given the all-clear to return to our rooms."

All windows were blacked out to prevent a bombing, and a nightly 10:00 p.m. curfew was enforced. Any misdemeanors by individuals brought threats of several days of collective punishment—in the form of less rations, early curfews, and probable physical abuse.

Initially we were put in a large, damp basement room, in B block.

My father said, "They built strong cement walls to divide large rooms and in summer, bugs accumulated in the stores, and walls, and crawled into the beds. We took our beds and mattresses outside, and they would come and pump chemicals on the whole damn thing—to clear up the bugs. It was awful!"

"Yes—the walls were… it was a terrible place!" My mother agreed, shuddering. "Just outside our window they were building coal briquettes, and the dust killed me!" she said. "I was allergic to it. I developed such terrible sinuses that for *four* days my forehead used to be swollen, and the pain was agonizing. In the end, they had to send me out—to the General Hospital. I was put in a ward with more than fourteen patients—some from other camps, and others who were not internees."

Mummy's serious sinus problems led to remedial surgery performed by Japanese doctors. Medical supplies were extremely scarce, so a minimal amount of anesthetic was administered. "They did a good job" she said, "but I had no pain killers—only ice packs to ease the intense pain. I suffered and groaned for several days after the operation, and stayed in hospital for about a month, because I was so ill."

Luckily, the camp authorities realized how much my mother had suffered, and relocated us to the third floor in A block.


I recalled how hard it was for me—at age five—and for David and Sylvia, to understand why our mother went away for such a long time. We felt very insecure, and suffered from separation-anxiety during this, and later episodes, when any one of us was sent to hospital for a lengthy period. David developed a nervous habit of fingering or sucking on the pointed edge of his shirt collar. It took several years before he was able to break himself of the comfort derived from his addiction. I don't know how he coped when he wasn't wearing a shirt…


My mother still corresponded sporadically with her friend, Prissy. "She was a *very* loving, darling girl," she said, "and we arranged by code, practically, that she would come and visit me in the hospital, and she did! As a neutral, she could enter and leave freely. She passed by the ward door, just made a sign, and winked at me. I followed her—we said we'd meet in the big toilet there. It was nice and clean…"

This obviously meant a lot to Mummy—*anywhere* was better than camp!

"She brought me something from her little, little allotment of food—a bean cake. It was so sweet of her. We cried on each other's shoulders. Then, Prissy offered me money. 'I have money in the bank,' she said, 'knocking around, doing nothing. Let me give it to you.'" My mother was emotional, remembering her friend's generosity and bravery. "I was overwhelmed, and said, 'No, no, no! I can't take it. Thank you.' And then she went *her* way, and I went mine. If she had been caught the Japanese would have beaten the life out of her!

"Prissy was a wonderful sportswoman," she reminded me. "We played volleyball, basketball, badminton, and swam together. Actually, until the last week before camp we were singing, *we're going into camp, we're going into camp.*"

I could *never* forget our last meeting with Prissy at Chaklianne's. "You sang that without realizing how bad camp would be?" I asked.

"Yes—we thought we'd be inside about six months," my mother replied.

Fifty years after the war, I attended an Old China Hands reunion in Las Vegas. A lady ran to me and looked at my nametag. "I knew it, I knew it—you're Liza's daughter!" she cried excitedly. "You look just like your mother." It was Prissy. After half a century they are once again in touch, since sadly losing contact completely when each left China, one for the United States, the other for Israel.

The internees were really very well organized and all were assigned duties—which they did willingly, most of the time. "Did everyone pull their weight?" I asked my mother.

"They *had* to! Everyone had something to do, except very old people who were sick, or something. People had kitchen duties, coal duties, making little briquettes for fuel, looking after the grounds, cleaning the place— it was kept hygienically clean all the time. The diseases that eventually affected the people had nothing to do with any dirt."

"Who organized it—the camp committee?" I asked.

"Yes—we had to look after it ourselves. You see—the Japanese ran the place, but the Commissioner of Police was head over everything. It was *very* well run. The stores had people looking after them—everything was weighed very fairly."

"Is that why the morale of the camp was high?" I asked.

"Yes. We had a very high morale," Mummy said, with pride.

"Do you think the other camps were *as* organized?"

"Not as highly as we were. Some of them had more squabbles, more troubles, all sorts of things… We heard it all later on."

Mummy worked several hours a week in the children's kitchen. Daddy, who was tall and able-bodied, worked in the coal shed, pushing wheelbarrows, stoking fires for cooking, and dishing out boiling water for very early morning and late afternoon tea, to patiently-waiting long queues. There was much to be done in the way of cleaning, gardening, maintenance and other necessary jobs. Like everyone else, he helped wherever he was needed.

"Did you think of yourselves as POWs?"

"Well I'll tell you—I saw it differently. I saw it as a kind of… " My mother was groping for the right words. "…I saw it as something we lived through which few people could experience. It was an experience—that's why I sort of studied it for myself each day. And I enjoyed it—I thought to myself, *what can I do that I can help with? What can I do to make it more fun also? Not to notice… to despair…* "

"Was that the general feeling among people—to help each other?"

"Yes," she said, "a lot of them. Only a very few neurotic, or really ill people, didn't."

# FIRST DAYS IN CAMP

From the first day at Yu Yuen Road camp, David and I shot away from our parents and went exploring. Sylvia, only two years old, was always with Mummy. When left on our own in the room and droning airplanes approached, we knew the distressing, whining sound would soon be followed by the thunderous noise of bombs exploding.

We dove under the table for shelter, shouting over and over, "The Jams are coming, the Jams are coming." This slang terminology was our secret code. It was really terrifying.

For years following the war, I had nightmares in which I ran and jumped over hurdles while being pursued by Japanese soldiers. I always awoke sweating, with my heart pounding.

I chewed on my nails until my fingers were bleeding and raw. This was a habit I picked up from watching our friend, Mrs. Hamovich, biting her nails when she came, always accompanied by her Amah, to visit us in our apartment, before our internment. Somehow, she managed to talk, drink tea, eat something, and indulge her habit, all at the same time. It took years for me to break the disgusting cycle of biting, mostly exacerbated by stress and fear.

Because hot water was in very short supply, we adhered to strict bathing hours allocated to men, women and children. Many took a bath at the same time in a large room with a stone floor. We had to wait in line for a turn. Mummy said, "We were allowed big buckets of hot water for our children's bath, one extra every day, so we bathed daily." Young children bathed in a large unattached galvanized-iron basin, sharing the same water whenever possible. The basin was emptied and refilled with water carried from boilers. We wore colorful Chinese wooden clogs that prevented slipping on the wet, soapy floor of the steamy bathing-room.

Mummy was one of a small group of privileged people who, because they did kitchen duty, could shower or take a real bath in hot water, in a round, deep, Chinese ceramic bathtub. One afternoon in summer, right after she had taken what she described as her "lovely bath," she went outside to the camp gardens. "I used some new soap sent by my mother in one of the few small parcels we were allowed," she said, "and it had a lovely scent. I went out alone. It was about four o'clock, and the weather was beautiful—I loved that time of day. We always went out to play softball."

Suddenly, Mummy was aware that a huge, dark green and black beetle was showing an uncommon interest in her. "It wouldn't leave me alone, so I started running away from it." Undeterred, the beetle chased her all the way across a large field to T Camp—quite a distance away from A Block. "The blooming beetle went into my clothes—I was screaming and shaking myself," Mummy said. "I was bending, jumping, and running around in circles, to no avail!"

I asked her what kind of beetle it was. "I think it was a Dung beetle—beautiful looking thing, but I still shiver when I see one!" she said.

"Dung beetle?"

"Yes—they're fierce—God! I was so scared. Something awful, awful, awful!" Mummy shuddered, imagining it again.

"Why do you think it was following you?" I was intrigued.

"Probably because it was attracted to the soap's scent."

Considering a Dung beetle's preference for what its name implies, I find it enigmatic that the persistent bug was enamored of the perfumed soap!

Some people watching her "frantics" were probably hysterical with laughter at this point. Eventually, they beat and killed the beetle while it was clinging to Mummy's back! I think they would have enjoyed watching her battle the bug a while longer, before relieving her of her misery!

"To this day I get chills up and down my spine, just thinking of it," she said. "I had many nightmares in which I was the featured star in the Beetle Chase!"

Luckily, Yu Yuen Road camp, once a well-equipped school, had the usual game fields and tennis courts. Mummy took in a whole bag of tennis balls, and games were played until the balls were thread-thin and rackets lost their punch. Nothing was replaced when it was used up.

There were only about three Jewish families in our camp, with no child my age. I had to deal daily with a large dose of anti-Semitism. I was left out of many events, unless it was expedient to have me in a team. Although rather petite, I was always keenly, actively interested in sports, even managing somehow to hold my own when teased or taunted by my peers.

On one occasion, several children followed me up a wide staircase, pushing me, pulling my hair and calling me names. "You killed Jesus," they accused. In the melee, one girl tumbled down the steps and suffered from mild concussion, for which I was blamed. I never heard the end of it!

"*Benjamimi-how, is a big fat cow,*" was the favorite chant of my relentless tormentors. They ganged up, poking me with hands and sticks. There was no escape. Although so unfairly matched, I fought back as bravely as I could.

"*Sticks and stones,*" I responded with pretended bravado, "*can break my bones, but names can never hurt me!*"

But of course they hurt—and continued to hurt for many years following the war.

"Turn the other cheek," Mummy advised consistently. "Don't show how much they hurt you. They'll soon stop if they think you don't care. Brush it off your shoulders!"

I was simply unable to master the art of *turning the other cheek,* and remained disconsolate.

Once, I was the only little girl left out of a child's birthday party. Why wasn't I invited? I couldn't understand it. Broken-hearted, and in childish defiance of my mother's orders, I decided to attend anyway. Since she had no knowledge of my clandestine intention, I wore my singlet, a vest, and took a handful of colorful buttons as a gift. All the children were dressed in party-clothes. Only one birthday cake and some cookies were on the table. I shriveled with embarrassment and pain when I encountered their hostile stares, and left almost immediately. The birthday child's mother lost no time complaining to Mummy, who scolded me soundly for putting her on the spot.

My parents never experienced the same overt anti-Semitism. Mummy's popularity, and many creative contributions to the internees were too valuable to be jeopardized.

Everyone was skinny and constantly hungry, but morale was boosted by innovative ideas, and regularly produced stage shows in which Mummy played a major role. She wrote scripts, choreographed the dancing, and always cheered everyone up with her wonderful ideas. Willing volunteers produced props and colorful costumes from scraps and various found items.

I had my first stage debut, did a back-bend, flopped ungracefully, and brought the house down in laughter!

## MAKING THE BEST OF IT

There was no serious crime or traffic threat in the incarceration area, so children of all ages roamed around freely. We played hopscotch, marbles, and skipped with pieces of rope internees had used to tie their belongings. We loved *stone, paper, scissors*, and played a game of skill with little bags full of stones and sand, instead of beans, that we threw and caught in mid-air. From the sounds of children's laughter at play, it was hard to believe the hunger, hardship, and deprivation we endured on a daily basis. The adults protected us from stress as best they could, under the circumstances.

I loved dressing up in found bits of white cloth that served as aprons and headscarves, to play "Doctors and Nurses." But I was often excluded, and stood nearby, wistfully watching the children—waiting to be invited to play again.

The sports fields and tennis courts were always fully occupied with informal, known or newly invented games, and organized sports competitions. We played a hiding game, the details of which have escaped my memory, in which the command "Olly, olly, oxi, all set FREE!" released us. I loved leapfrog, three-legged races and other running games. My favorite pastime was to hang on the horizontal bar as long as possible. When there was nothing else to do, I amused myself with somersaults, cartwheels, backbends and handstands.

When I could find a ball to play with, I would throw it against the wall, saying the words aloud in a singsong manner, while doing the actions described:

*Oliver Twist, can you do this?*
*Touch your knee, touch your toe*
*Turn around, and under you go*

I got really good at keeping control of the ball. Other children were always hanging around, waiting to pounce the minute it rolled out of my reach.

Large empty jam tins and other rationed food containers became stilts when the tops were punched with holes and threaded with strings. In winter, we filled the tins with paper, punched the sides full of holes, set the paper alight and ran into the wind, holding the tins close to our thinly clothed, emaciated bodies. It was blissful to feel the heat blow through for a few fleeting moments.

Because my peers excluded me from so many games and activities, I had a lot of solitary time on my hands. I cut cardboard paper dolls and clothed them in pretty, colorful clothes I designed and painted, using watercolors. I often helped watch over babies, and keep them amused. I rocked or wheeled strollers and prams, and was really popular with busy, overstressed, young mothers.

Despite precautions taken, inadequate maternity facilities, and whispers of abortions, some babies were indeed born in camp. They were always welcomed and fussed over. Doctors and nurses, also interned, did their best to help mother and child stay healthy. Everyone rose to the occasion, which signified renewed hope and life.

During the freezing winters the quadrangle developed a thin layer of ice and became an instant skating rink. We slid around on whatever we wore on our feet. When it snowed we made snowmen and threw snowballs. Our laughter was uplifting to all, and brought sad smiles to the faces of adults who watched us at play.

One summer's day Daddy introduced new joy into my life when he sat me on a garden bench, in the sunshine, and magically produced some wool and knitting needles. After my first patiently taught knitting lesson, I couldn't get enough of it, and used any colored scraps of wool I could find. Daddy also taught me how to "knit" a continuous tail through the hole of an old wooden bobbin, after he knocked four nails into the top of it. When I ran out of wool I simply unraveled my work and started over again.

We found ways in simple, creative enjoyment, to overcome our constant hunger and difficult circumstances.

Most of the time, after outgrowing the last of our tennis shoes, we ran barefoot. This freedom was the greatest contributor to my peasant's feet of today!

Long pants were remodeled into shorts and all other clothing was creatively refashioned to fit family members. All was eventually passed on for others to use until threadbare. Everything was recycled to death!

Mummy's entire family, the Jacobs, not being British, was not interned. But they, and all others with similar status, had to wear armbands, printed with a prominent black "X." They lived nearby, also on Yu Yuen Road.

Occasionally, my uncles, or some of our other relations, walked alongside the camp's high, steel picket fence. Great care was taken not to be too obvious. It was very dangerous to risk recognition by suspicious Japanese guards. David would kick the ball into the thicket up to the fence, and then, when he retrieved it, a look, and perhaps a word or two, would pass between him and our daring relatives.

Mummy would stand on the pathway beyond the bushes, calling, "David, Ester, Sylvia—are you OK? Be careful—don't go near the gate. Did you eat breakfast? Come and eat. Daddy is looking for you. I have to go to work in the kitchen now." Things like that—Mummy called it *double-wording*. "They understood, so they didn't make any signs," she said. "I was worried, because a few people were caught."

Through a few carefully chosen words and coded messages, she conveyed as much information as possible about our welfare and activities.

After a long, long time, we were allowed visitors. My grandfather came, and it was very emotional. "He was allowed to bring us a parcel— they were sending us little parcels regularly. Every February they were allowed to…" my mother said.

"Only once," my father interrupted, "end of 1943, they said, 'we'll let people come to see their families.'"

During that single permitted visit during our entire internment, my grandfather sat across from my mother at a little table and they held hands and cried. They hardly spoke.

Many teachers were interned in the various camps. Every morning we attended classes conducted under difficult conditions, with hardly any supplies, managing somehow with the meager amount of paper, pencils, erasers and rulers at our disposal. We shared everything, and took turns borrowing the few available storybooks. As a five-year-old, I was really too young to be aware of the tremendous achievement of our educators, despite their frustration and many adversities.

We lived a life of escapism, living vicariously through stories of fairytale characters. Which hungry child in camp wouldn't identify with Charles Dickens's *Oliver Twist*? Or feel moved during the Christmas season by *A Christmas Carol*, the tale of mean, miserly, old and bitter Ebenezer Scrooge? His redemption kept hope burning that good ultimately prevails over evil.

We listened intently, with saucer-wide eyes, to some rather terrifying, distressing stories with happy endings, all in a large book, titled "Grimm's Fairytales." Amongst them were, *Little Red Riding Hood, Hansel and Gretel, Snow White*, and *Cinderella*.

Hans Christian Andersen's wonderful tales, *The Snow Queen, The Emperor's New Clothes*, and *The Mermaid*, enchanted us. All the books were brought into camp by internees.

With the innocence and faith of childhood we believed, and hoped, a fairytale hero would suddenly appear to release us all from captivity! These stories, in multiple languages, are still widely read today by, or to, children who are mostly well-fed, free, safe, and perhaps securely tucked in bed.

Some newer children's books by Enid Blyton, who would eventually become one of England's most beloved and prolific authors, soon appeared. The first of *The Famous Five* Series, *Five on a Treasure Island*, somehow arrived in camp. I loved them, and continued well into my teen years to be an avid reader of her exciting adventure and mystery stories.

Once, returning to school with one of our precious, scarce schoolbooks I had taken home when it was my turn, I went into the hastily erected, huge, ramshackle hut that hid the open-pit toilets. Suddenly, somehow, I lost my grip on the book, and watched in horror and dismay as it fell and made a loud plopping sound before slowly sinking into the cesspool beneath my shaking, frightened little body.

As horrifying as that was for me, it was better than the fate of a couple of internees who actually fell into the pit, and had to be rescued and medically treated! They were absolutely traumatized by the experience. Never was the phrase, *There, but for the grace of God, go I*, more applicable, or sobering!

Even today, I find it extremely difficult to discard my huge hoard of surplus reading and writing material. I probably have more pens, pencils, crayons, and erasers in mugs and jars, and new writing paper taking up shelf space and storage bins, than the total shared in our camp schoolrooms!

## MAIZE AND SOYBEAN MILK

On Mummy's kitchen-duty days, the children always ran into the dining room saying eagerly, "It's Mrs. Benjamin's day today. Yummy!" During our entire internment, Mummy never tasted the non-kosher meat dishes she created. She taught her kitchen helpers to prepare tasty Sephardic-style dishes with the few spices and ingredients at hand, and was an extremely popular cook.

"At first I was just chopping vegetables," Mummy said, "but naturally, when they found I could cook a bit more than the others I was collared into cooking for the children every six days. And, right away, Daddy was recruited into carting wheelbarrows of coal for the big kitchen stoves. We were given our rations—that were so small. Daddy was strait-laced—rigidly honest. When he was on duty I didn't dare go *near* the kitchen! He wouldn't even take a small onion. But there were others who took advantage…"

Mummy took the discarded heads of fish, tops of cabbages, carrots, and other available vegetables and dried them all with salt. These items, relegated to the rubbish heap, were cooked and often shared with friends who arrived to savor Mummy's delicious food.

She made sticky, sweet, peanut brittle, and baked trays and trays of cakes, using Japanese syrup called *Midzu-ame*. It was a clear, amber-colored, sticky, sugary liquid. Daddy referred to it as *sugar water*, and said, "It became like golden treacle. The Japanese brought it in, and every week they offered it for a higher price.

They said, 'I'll sell you a jar of 200lbs Midzu-ame'— and if you paid $1.00 for 300 grams a week before, the following week you would pay $1.50, or $1.70. If you asked "Why?" They always answered, 'The price has gone up.'"

The Swiss Consulate gave us each $10.00 spending allowance, so our family had $50.00. We had to buy sugar, peanut butter, and sundry items that were available in the canteen. We were also allowed to purchase a six, or eight-pack of cigarettes. The Japanese bought everything from the Chinese and brought it to camp. They were bringing in big washing soap that we bought for ex-amount per block. It was a very rough quality and just about shredded our hands! We also received camp soap, and did our washing on galvanized iron washing boards in huge troughs.

There were two other families who kept kosher—one big family, and one young man. We looked after each other, and we all linked up together when there was a holiday.

"Was there ever any question in your mind about breaking the kosher law?" I wanted to know.

"Never, never!" Mummy said. "I let the children eat, because I knew one thing—they were giving the best meat to the children, and I didn't question that. I would never let the kids be harmed in any way. You were growing and your bones would be weak, so I let you all eat the food. Every six days, when I cooked, I saw what they had. They gave the kids quite good treatment because essentially, the Japanese believed in favoring children— when they talked about them they said, 'Ah! Children—they're like God!'"

We were each allotted a little plot and people started growing some vegetables. But suddenly we found all the radishes we grew had vanished, so it was a hopeless case. People stole it during the night!

We ate yellow maize, ground by internees, and drank soybean milk produced from crushed and strained raw beans. The Japanese were unaware of the actual good food value of these particular items. Mummy often entrusted me with frying the once-weekly egg ration. We ate stale, rotting black cabbages and potatoes, and had no fruits. Large marrowbones made good, but thin soup, and imaginative ideas of the cooks produced some rather surprisingly tasty dishes.

Every day around noon large wicker baskets, full of bread made from cracked wheat flour, were brought in. Each internee was allowed a loaf, so our family got five. The children couldn't eat their whole loaf, so something was always left over. The bread had to be eaten fresh and hot, because by evening it was like cement. My parents cut the bread and put the slices on the kitchen stove—they could go there any time they wanted because the cooks, all fellow internees, were their friends.

Sometimes bachelors, or old women, would eat their loaves and have none left, but were still hungry. They would go around with a small basket and ask, "Who has any bread you don't need?" And people would give them their surplus.

Bachelors took advantage of the fact that they could trade with the Japanese—for a watch, or for butter, whisky, and various other items— especially during Christmas and New Year. Some guards were friendly with men whom they knew from outside, before internment. They would go into their quarters to play a game of cards. "Good morning, good morning. How are you? Ah—very nice—very nice!" they would say, politely, almost using up their entire English vocabulary with these few words!

A few Eurasian internees with British passports had a Japanese parent, and spoke Japanese.

"The British policemen, officers who were in camp with us, used to slowly stroll along the walls, trying to be unnoticed," my father recalled. "Then, a Chinese police constable, or someone outside who knew the British officer, (who was their superior before camp) comes up and makes some sort of sign. He might pass the officer a small slip of paper, or say something like, *"Allies attacked so-and-so."* You understand what I mean? It was very dangerous—the Japanese must never see this happening."

"The Chinese outside giving to the British inside." I said.

"Yes. Because the Chinese outside had many neutral subjects who never went to camp."

"So these British were actually intelligence?" I probed.

"No! They were inside. They got news for us. They said, 'You know what happened in Europe and so-and-so, in Singapore, Australia?' Maybe news that we sank a number of Japanese ships… you understand?

"Somebody outside with a ham radio, or something like that, tuned in to BBC, or elsewhere, and could get information from far away. He gave it to the Chinese, and *they* passed us the information. But—if *one* man is caught in camp, he gets the hiding of his life. He's put down on his knees, his hands tied behind him, and they beat him on the neck, like the Japanese jugular vein."

"Were there a lot like that?" I asked, horrified by this revelation.

"Quite a few were caught," my father said, "and every time one man did something wrong like that, the whole camp would be punished. Like, one month no entertainment, six o'clock in the evening lights go out, or they wouldn't allow the Swiss Consul to deliver rations. Because of one man!"

"Was he punished publicly?"

"No! He gets a beating—or something similar. Or they take him away to Bridge House—Japanese interrogation—and there he stays, getting the beating of his life. Maybe he comes back, or he doesn't. We don't know what happened to him…" My father says sadly.

"Often, at inspection time in the evening," my father continued, "a Japanese police officer would come with the Consular police—a foreign superior or something. Then the Japanese would say 'It's New Year time now. You want me to bring you something?' So you ask 'What?' and he says, 'Give me your watch, and I'll bring you two bottles of whisky'—or something similar. But, it's done in such a hush-hush way…

"Now—if a boy, after six months, slowly thinks he's had enough and can't stand any more, he quietly dresses up at night, slips through the mud, and under the barbed wire. He gets out. There are Chinese outside who will take him into Hangzhou and smuggle him into Chungking, to join the forces. We had such cases. Our friend Evelyn's brother was smuggled out and became a captain. Another one in our camp also went out. They all went to Chungking. There were three forces—Chiang Kai-shek…" My father left the rest of the sentence hanging in the air.

"Was everyone punished when someone escaped like that?"

"Yes—the punishment was: no more rations picked up this time, no more parcels from American Red Cross."

"What was in the parcels?" I remembered the parcels but not the details.

"Butter, sugar, coffee, jam, all sorts of things. They were called *One-in-ten*."

I had no idea why the parcels were thus named. Now I asked, "And we had roll calls every morning?"

"Every morning and evening," my father stated.

"At what time?"

"About eight o'clock in the morning—outside the door. Just before people ate breakfast and went out. Around six or seven o'clock in the evening."

"And that was for everybody? Children as well?"

"Yes. All standing in line."

I remembered standing in rows for roll calls in the assembly hall. The pictures were still vividly etched in my own memory. "Now, if you were sick, could you…"

"When I was sick in bed, with this bleeding business, they asked, 'Where's your husband?' Liza said, 'Inside, sick.' The Japanese said, 'Stay in bed—stay in bed!'"

"Did everyone eat breakfast in a communal place?"

"No! Bachelors ate their food in the men's dormitory and spinsters and single girls ate in the women's dormitory."

"How many people were in the camp—do you know?" As an adult I would understand a head count. As a child we seemed surrounded by multitudes of hungry, thin people. I was about to find out my perception was correct.

"We had around 1,000, or more. We had three buildings—big grounds."

"What was your daily routine? You had light cooking duties…"

"Everybody was appointed to some job. If a man was a good shoemaker, for example, they put him in place fixing shoes, and so on."

"And he never changed it—that was his job—shoemaker?"

"Yeah. And he knew what to do—your shoes. We bartered, 'Hey folks—give me a packet of cigarettes,' or something like that… When you called a carpenter, he came in and you'd say, 'Fix me a couple of shelves…' He'd say, 'Ok—what do I get for that? Cocoa—or two packets of cigarettes?' Something like that…"

"Why did you end up only doing cooking duty?"

"Because I was thinking of getting into that so as not to do harder work. What else would I do? For me, peeling potatoes is nothing."

"You did that every day?"

"No— once every four days—one long fourteen-hour day. Every now and then they'd give me a big saucepan to wash—pork saucepans…"

I imagined how difficult this must have been for my religiously observant father. I didn't dare pursue this subject any further! "Then what did you do on the other days?" I asked, tactfully shifting tracks.

"Wash your napkins, and washed bed sheets, and washed every bloody thing…" he answered, half in jest.

"Did they have anything like handicraft or sewing classes in camp?"

"Not organized classes—among themselves. And even then, they took money and cigarettes," my father said.

"Women got together and made clothes," my mother added, "and they also gave ballet lessons. They took money and everything."

During our second year in camp, the Abrahams, a large, religiously observant family, were transferred from Lunghwa to Yu Yuen Road. Mrs. Abraham was expecting a baby and had to be near a hospital. She also needed a milk supply for herself and the newborn. One daughter remained behind in Lunghwa to continue studying nursing.

Mr. Abraham told the camp representative, who was previously the Shanghai Commissioner of Police, that his wife was expecting. "What do you think this is?" The representative asked, "The Country Club?"

"I'm not asking your permission," Mr. Abraham replied. "I'm letting you know—this is just information for you."

Their son, Abe, told me, "At first I worked in garbage detail—picking up the garbage, morning and evening. I liked it," he said, "because I had all day free to myself. But then, I got an eye infection—conjunctivitis—from the dust and kitchen ashes. The camp doctors told me I couldn't do that job any more.

"Then, there was this job in the kitchen—I was seventeen years old at that time, and in my life I never handled raw meat—especially meat that was not Kosher! I just couldn't handle it, and after one week I gave up that job and went into fixing shoes. I learnt that in camp.

"We used to have prayers every Saturday, and every holiday," he remembered, "and one thing I must tell you—people think the Japanese were anti-Semitic, and they were not at all. In fact Hayashi was very good to us."

Abe said, "My brother and I started a Boy Scout Troop. We made uniforms and badges… First of all, in Shanghai we were very active in the scouts—both of us were gold-cord wearers, which means we had 'so many' badges." He was the scoutmaster and I was his assistant."

Some ex-internees related with authority and conviction that dog meat was served to the adults. Mummy swears she never saw any during her duties in the children's kitchen. Fortunately, my parents never ate meat during internment.

Daddy worried enough about our lack of nutrition to regularly line us children up against the wall and force-feed us spoonfuls of tasteless, colorless, slippery intestinal "stew." I remember gagging, and even vomiting, but he was relentless. Although drastic, in the long run this measure was really nourishing and good for us.

"I used to—sort of—make you eat meat with all the grit and that kind of stuff," my father said, "because I knew that if you didn't have this in your body you'd have nothing at all. You'd go out half dead."

"I remember that," I said, "standing up and eating. We had to eat that food. Ugh! How often did that happen—every day?" I asked. I could still dredge up the awful memory—so many years after the war!

"Almost every day. I used to give you food by force to make you strong—otherwise, only God could help you."

"Why," I asked my father, "do I remember black cabbage and potatoes, and other bad food, so vividly?"

"Because the cooks used Chinese sauce. Of course, children also had difficulties to overcome. Sometimes parents and four children were all crammed together in one room. The kids never had a proper meal—never had anything like ice cream or cakes. Never went to a cinema. They had nothing to make them feel they had any enjoyment. They just ate pieces of meat and Japanese rice-boiled congee—and nothing else. A few beans and strips of meat... that's not what a kid, or anybody, would like to eat every day—for three, four, or five years."

Victor, a fellow internee told me, "Once, in the adult dining hall, the rice dished out was bright pink! The cook on duty ran out wringing his hands and pleading, 'Please don't worry about the rice. You can eat it— there's nothing wrong with it!'" The bottom of the pan revealed a pair of drained red socks that had originally been hung above the stove to dry! No one claimed ownership, but the hilarity it created for days was well worth the anxiety felt by the first people who received the pink rice!

When possible, internees bartered services for food rations and other items. Mummy cut hair for a little jam or other tidbits. She was self-taught, and still regularly cuts her own hair.

Fear made us all bed-wetters until well past average age. I don't think much was understood about childhood trauma, so parents didn't handle the problem very kindly. Daddy was a stern disciplinarian and we were terrified when we "slipped." His father's tragic suicide in 1935 had set him back emotionally. Overwhelmed by his own problems, frustration and fear—for us, and for his mother and siblings incarcerated in Pootung, another Shanghai camp—he was often morose, depressed, intolerant and short- tempered. Sometimes he lashed out uncontrollably. It took great skill to dodge painful blows to our heads and bodies.

Sadly, Daddy's moods masked his great sense of humor and we welcomed the moments when he would keep us all laughing, in spite of our difficult circumstances and uncertain future.

# HELL'S BELLS

Commandant Hashimoto, accompanied by an entourage of soldiers, attended Mummy's show—*Hell's Bells*, a tongue-in cheek send-up of *Dante's Inferno*. In a bizarre way, he was proud of his camp's achievements and showed off by inviting officers from other camps to attend performances. All wore uniforms and decorations, sat in the front row, and applauded loudly and appreciatively.

The production was a huge success that played to packed audiences. "I had thirty-two people taking part in the whole show." Mummy said. "It ran for three nights. The first night was quite nicely full, the second night people sat on windowsills, and stood at the back of the hall, or anywhere they found a spot to squeeze into. The third night, the Japanese Commandant, and even the priests came to see it—because it had something to do with hell. Everybody was laughing!"

The tallest lady in camp, cast as the "Queen of Hell," claimed the shortest little man—whom she caught in her arms as he was thrown into the inferno for his sins—as her lover. Daddy, cast as a Rabbi, was hilarious and brought the house down. There was a lot of acting, dancing and singing, and anyone who had talent, or a longing to be on stage, was in the show. Some had been professional entertainers before internment.

After stripping the meat from all the huge marrowbones they gave us for making soup, the bones were dried on the rooftops and used as the devils' instruments for clacking, while chanting, *Humba, Tutta, Lo, Lo,*

*Humba, Tutta, Lo, Lo.*

The day after the performance, the Japanese Commandant, Hashimoto, invited Mummy up to his office and wanted her to give him dancing lessons. "Prease—Mrs. Benjamin," he said politely, his tight smile exposing yellowing teeth, "I would rike to rearn to dance. Can you give me dancing ressons?"

"I was taken completely by surprise, and really frantic with fear," Mummy said, "but, thank God, very soon after, they were so bothered with the war situation that he forgot all about it. That's how it slowly fizzled out…"

Before the war Mummy taught English to Japanese soldiers. It seemed the Japanese—probably because they already had their war agenda in place—realized the importance of understanding the enemy's language.

We all loved communal dance sessions in which *The Hokey-pokey* and *Lambeth Walk* were great favorites. We sang *It's a Long Way to Tiperary, Danny Boy, When Irish Eyes Are Smiling,* and other popular songs. It took our minds off our difficult prison life and helped enormously to raise everyone's spirits.

Our theme song, *The First Five Years in a Shanghai C.A.C.* (Civil Assembly Centre), was first sung in a camp stage review in 1944, and soon became a regular at performances and other occasions. The raised voices of our stoic internees portrayed their indomitable spirit and fortitude as they sang:

*It's the first five years,*
*Just the first five years,*
*That's the hardest time of all;*
*If you can smile and sing*
*While the queue-bells ring,*
*You can answer any call.*
*There's plenty of work, and little money,*
*But there's really no cause for any worry;*
*And the future's bright for you and me,*
*It's the first five years,*
*That's the hardest, Dears,*
*In a Shanghai C.A.C.*

In the evenings, meeting friends and socializing was permitted. My father said, "We were quite free—we weren't in a prison. After working hours we went from one room to another. We knew our friends from the gardens and fields; we would talk together—play a game or something.

"Around nine o'clock the lights would go out and everyone had to go back to their room and put a small light on, or maybe sit down in the dimly-lit corridor and talk. We were not allowed to smoke when we came out, because they were afraid an allied plane would see light…"

I recalled our blacked-out windows. We had a young friend, David, who used to come to our room on Friday night, or Jewish holidays. He was Mummy's childhood friend Aliza's brother. He took a risk in coming to us, but my father said, "He lived in the bachelors' room. He didn't run away—they knew he always came to our room because he was our Jewish friend."

There were some priests and religious groups in camp who organized all sorts of events. We Jewish people were few, and had no organizations, so we looked after ourselves. When we had our holidays we were sent in some things, such as *matzoth* for Passover. Sometimes Mummy baked the matzoth herself.

On Friday evening, before sunset, Mummy always lit homemade Sabbath candles. As her own mother and maternal ancestors had always done, she rubbed cotton wool between her palms until she had two strands, which she put into an oil base. The candles continued to flicker and burn for a long while, throwing dancing shadows across walls as the thin strands waved slightly. We sat in semi darkness and recanted the Sabbath prayer over bread and wine, or its substitute.

There was always something to eat. As usual, Mummy made something out of nothing much. In these simple ways the spirit and hope of our culture was maintained.

"Where is Li-li?" I ask Mummy insistently. But she is unable to answer with certainty.

Sylvia, seriously ill with pneumonia, was taken away a couple of weeks ago to an unknown, unnamed hospital destination. She stood at the back of the truck, arms outstretched, howling. Mummy tried, despite extreme pain and anxiety, to reassure Li-li by waving "goodbye" bravely, until the truck was out of sight. Only then did she allow herself to break down in floods of tears.

I miss my little sister very much, and am unable to comprehend why she's staying away so long. Everyone is sad, but they have no answers.

Mummy always sings to Sylvia—*Velia, Oh Velia, the Nymph of the Night*… Now her voice is silent. She doesn't even sing my song—*Oh Rose Marie I love you, I'm always dreaming of you…* Rosemary is my middle name. She's just not in the mood.

There was no word from authorities about Sylvia's condition or whereabouts. It was mid-winter, with bitingly cold, freezing temperatures. Her immune system was extremely weakened, thanks to the lack of heating and inadequate medical facilities.

Mummy and Daddy are beside themselves with worry. And scared to voice their secret fears.

Our family is carrying on with daily life and duties as best we can, under the circumstances. Caring friends try to reassure us. "Sylvia will soon be back—don't worry. No one has disappeared yet without word, after being hospitalized."

Nothing would help but Li-li's reappearance—and she did reappear suddenly—several weeks after being whisked away! No word preceded her arrival. What joy and relief!

Too young to give a full account of what actually happened during her absence, years later Sylvia said, "I was forcibly and mercilessly torn from my parents' arms, forced to stand on the back of an open army truck, and taken to an unknown destination. A fear of separations and abandonment, as well as recurring nightmares of the experience, have accompanied me most of my life. I returned from hospital with a lung problem that lasted several decades."

Everyone made a fuss of Sylvia. Mummy and Daddy, blissfully thankful for her safe return, watched over her with extreme love, caring, and bouts of anxiety. No one wanted a repeat of the past agonizing month of separation and unvoiced fears.

# YANGTZEPOO CAMP

A few months before the end of the war, we were stunned by the announcement we were to be relocated to Yangtzepoo, a new, hastily set-up camp. It was actually a long-condemned, derelict cluster of Japanese military hospital buildings, mortuary, and squad barracks that formerly belonged to a religious order. Now it was doubling as an undercover arms and ammunition depot. Aware that the Allies had targeted it for bombing, our captors strategically relocated us, hoping we would be inadvertent victims. They probably theorized it would give them some protection from further Allied attacks on other Japanese positions.

The move from Yu Yuen Road to Yangtzepoo, about nine miles away, was extremely difficult and stressful. A major operation, it meant dismantling our well-established infrastructure, transferring our personal belongings, and shifting all indoor and outdoor camp equipment. Irreplaceable pharmaceutical products from the clinic and dispensary, all kitchen utensils, library books and anything else of value had to be crated up carefully. It was all too precious to lose.

When we moved they took us first by tram, and then crammed us into open trucks. We endured a bumpy, uncomfortable drive. About a mile from our destination, with no apparent motive other than suddenly satisfying a sadistic sense of fun, they removed a truckload of women and children, old and young, and forced them to walk the rest of the way. The streets were lined with a few free foreigners amidst dense crowds of noisy, jeering Chinese, all watching an incongruous parade. With great difficulty Mummy carried my four-year-old sister most of the way. We all carried stuff. We walked, and walked, and walked, in convoy with everyone else. It was like a walking caravan. It was a *long* way. We were exhausted… our trunks and everything else were brought in separately."

"Did you know where we were going? Were you frightened?" I asked my mother.

"No—I don't know why we were never frightened," she said. "We knew that we were going to another camp—to a Japanese squad barracks. There was a part where we had to go past, but not *into* the ex-Japanese soldiers' camp."

Thankfully, the sun was shining and the weather was in our favor. Once again, chaos reigned when we found all our baggage and equipment scattered outside the main gate. To our dismay, we discovered we were to be combined—in a smaller area than we had vacated—with another camp that had been moved from Pootung, on the other side of the river.

A pre-fabricated Japanese temple stood a few paces from the entrance. We sneaked a peek in and saw it was resplendent with idols, incense, and other colorful temple paraphernalia like those I had last seen before our internment.

The dilapidated buildings, slated for demolition before the war, had been taken over by rats. Bugs were found crawling in the walls. All plumbing facilities were covered in dirt and in a dreadful state of disrepair. Filthy toilets were blocked and took days to fix. Out of necessity, a row of field-type latrines had to be dug to cope with the numbers sharing the seriously inadequate facilities.

Every evening, at twilight, volumes of dark, ugly bats appeared everywhere, and flew around just above our heads, adding to our discomfort in the barren surroundings. They proliferated in the entire city, frightening everyone. Mummy was so scared she wore a headscarf whenever she was outside in the evening. We were told bats could get into your hair and were impossible to remove! I never heard of it happening, and suspect it was a myth, but was happy it wasn't ever put to the test!

Unlike Yu Yuen Road, the new camp only had one kitchen, so mealtimes had to be staggered, entailing a lot more work for the kitchen staff. Our meals were usually the same—watered down yellow maize or *congee* (rice) for breakfast, rice or—rarely—potatoes, cabbage, and a little meat for lunch, with a duplication of the same for dinner. Frozen carcasses were delivered in a skinned and decapitated condition, but one day, two carcasses had heads and tails of mongrel dogs attached! No one really wanted to know what we were eating. Our family never suffered through that ordeal—because of Jewish dietary observance.

I've heard Ribbonfish, a nickname for a fish that was approximately one-and-a-half inches wide and four feet long, was another protein staple. I don't personally recall seeing, or eating it.

On the very first day at Yangtzepoo, I, "The Fearless Child Explorer," went into a dry, overgrown field flanking the buildings, and discovered a little outhouse—obviously a latrine—in the middle of nowhere. I opened the door and almost jumped out of my skin when a loudly squawking chicken flew into the air. I slammed the door shut and ran home with a pounding heart to announce, "I found a chicken! I found a chicken!" I shouted and hopped around. My parents were convinced I had taken leave of my senses!

Unfortunately, we were unable to perform the ritualistic kosher slaughtering, so the chicken was a delicious treat for someone else!

The camp committee wasted no time reorganizing and re-delegating duties and work. Every afternoon many of us watched our men dig a huge, deep hole in the ground. Finally, after many days, they reached water. The joy was immeasurable at finding this source that would soon irrigate the vegetable patches we planted and tended with such loving care.

A flimsy, dull-colored curtain separated us from a newly wed young couple with whom we shared a very big room in a rickety building, which was a barracks.

From the start, it was obvious we were badly matched with our roommates, and things came to a head when we children were ill with jaundice and dysentery, the dreaded endemic disease. The *honeymooners* complained angrily when they could no longer stand our fighting and crying.

Mummy said, "You kids were so incontinent, and couldn't control— never mind... You wanted to go to the toilet three or four times at night, and it was awful... we had a little potty in the room, because we couldn't very well go right out of the place in the dark—way out—through the little fields, to get to the toilet. And it was very dangerous at night. You could fall through very easily!"

Then, horror of horrors! One night, in the dark, one of us accidently knocked our colorful, hand-painted Chinese chamber-potty over, spilling the night's contents. They flowed inexorably under the curtain into the enemy's quarters. It was the last straw!

"The man was so angry," Mummy told me. "We were apologetic, but what could we do? It was an accident. The next day, he waited for Daddy to come back from early morning kitchen duty. Those days he was looking after the fire and all that, from five o'clock, so he was exhausted—and all black on his face. He was wearing clogs because there were no more shoes left. The man waited near our door, and when Daddy came he said, "I have a word to say to you!"

"Sure," Daddy said, "please come in."

"No!" he said, and right away gave Daddy a punch on the jaw. Then they had a terrible fistfight in the passage outside our room. We stood with several others who gathered in the wide corridor, and watched in horror as Daddy and his adversary battered each other, fiercely inflicting blows and wounds they probably wished on our Japanese captors.

"But Daddy was the bigger man; the other fellow thought that he would get the better of the fight by starting it off," Mummy said. "And then, everybody came, took them outside, and formed a ring. They had a *helluva* boxing and wrestling competition! The other fellow was terribly battered. Because he won, Daddy rode him in the end, and it was very funny!"

"His name was Sammy Jones," Daddy interjected.

The commandant thought it better to remove us from there, "Because," he said, "It's very difficult for this couple to understand probrems with chirdren."

They moved us to one of the newer buildings, originally built for the army. The Japanese commandant was living on the top floor, and we were given a quiet room on the second floor.

"Very few people were there—it was all empty and a little frightening, but it wasn't so bad, just the same," Mummy said, "so we lived in a nice, much stronger room."

When we were in the first rickety building and bombs were falling, Mummy prepared a "cave of trunks" by placing two of our trunks side by side, with a gap in between, and covering them with another huge trunk on top. "Come on," she said, "we're hiding in our cave of trunks." We went into the "shelter" and sang our favorite songs. "We had fun," she said, with her usual ability to see the bright side, "and afterwards we went about our business, and it was tremendous!"

David discovered a cesspool near some ramshackle, flattish

buildings—the original mortuary. He picked up a long pole and plunged it in to measure its depth. The next minute I was horrified to see him fall, and begin sinking fast in the black, muddy sludge. I grabbed him, and somehow, fear gave me enough strength to pull him out. There was a large basin in a washing-room near the mortuary. It was probably used to wash bodies—or things connected to the dead and dying. I never gave it a second thought! I scrubbed his blackened, muddy shirt, hoping I could get it clean enough to keep the episode a secret from our parents! As a young child, my priorities were not yet in the best order, and I never realized how grateful they would be that David had survived a near-tragedy.

Close to the cesspool, we watched in fascination as kids poked around and dug up some human skulls and other fragments of human remains, and small personal trinkets. I guess we were the first "self-styled archaeologists" of a Japanese mortuary!

David built a raft with some pieces of wood he found near the broken-down buildings. We all watched as he completed and sailed it across one of three man-made, oblong fishing ponds. We never saw any fish—only an abundance of mosquitoes, tadpoles and frogs. Any diversion was welcomed, and we created adventures out of thin air. Innovation at all levels was the order of the day. Kite-flying, claimed as a Chinese invention, was a favorite pastime. There were no real sporting facilities, so any activity that space permitted in the new camp was encouraged and pursued.


Everyone was very worried about the rumored bombing of our camp. We had an extremely efficient underground network going. I followed David and some other children onto a flat rooftop of one of the buildings and watched our men dip brushes into deep buckets of white lime. They painted POW, large X's, and coded messages, alerting allied pilots of our presence. It was really quite fantastic, and probably thanks to them the bombing was averted.

# BRIDGE HOUSE

More and more horrific accounts of Japanese atrocities began filtering through our networks. The scope of mass killings, raping, and torture of Chinese people was unimaginable and incomprehensible. Chinese and foreign victims alike suffered imprisonment and indescribable torture at Bridge House—the dreaded, infamous prison— just past Garden Bridge, on the Hongkew side. The name, spoken in hushed tones, sent chills of fear up one's spine. If they survived, few emerged from there without lifelong, serious, debilitating injuries and emotional disorders.

The prison, originally a multi-storied apartment building, was taken over by the *Kempeitai*—the dreaded Japanese military police—and converted into their headquarters and interrogation center. It had multiple torture chambers, and windowless cells shared by many inmates. Foreigners and Chinese, men and women, were crammed into a confined space, with only a bucket as a toilet and no bathing facilities. Rodents, roaches, lice, and bugs, ran rampant, spreading disease, dysentery, and misery.

The shrieks of those being tortured on higher floors could be heard clearly by those in the cells, striking them with unimaginable terror. They knew they too could be dragged out at any moment of night or day, to be interrogated and tortured. Some of the innovative methods used were immeasurably cruel—beatings with bamboo sticks on bare bodies of kneeling victims and burning private parts with cigarettes. Water torture was a Japanese favorite. A copious amount of water was poured into the victim's mouth and nostrils. Sometimes an interrogator jumped on his bloated stomach, or hanged the poor wretch upside down from the ceiling to drain him, before starting over again. Innumerable other horrific forms of torture were inflicted on detainees.

Initially, after the Battle of Shanghai in 1937, only Chinese prisoners were interrogated at Bridge House. After the Japanese takeover of the International Settlement, in 1941, westerners were also held there and subjected to the same rigorous maltreatment, deprivations, and tortures, as the Chinese with whom they shared the filthy, minuscule cells.

Detainees, if released—sometimes after extended periods of torture, and usually on the brink of death—were warned never to speak of their experiences at Bridge House if they wished to avoid immediate re-arrest.

The Japanese, like the Nazis, considered themselves a "master race" with unlimited power and self-awarded permission to perpetuate, with impunity, barbaric acts on a mammoth scale.

One morning, while standing at roll call, a fairly new, baboon-like guard with big shoulders and long arms, strutted arrogantly between the lines of internees. He held himself erect at full height, slightly short of five feet. Mummy was lost in thought and before she realized what was happening, the guard had stopped in front of her, and, with deliberation, touched her rudely on the chin with one pointed finger.

"Don't you dare to touch me!" Mummy's involuntary reaction horrified everyone. The little man, taken by surprise, seemed stunned and unable to deal with such unexpected bravery! After a moment, he walked away. We all breathed a sigh of relief.

"Liza," Daddy asked later, "how could you do such a thing? Do you know what they can do to you?" He was genuinely frightened, expecting imminent repercussions. Fortunately, as days and weeks went by, no mention was ever made of the incident. Soon after, the guard disappeared. The Camp Commandant—aware at this stage that Japan was not doing well on the battlefront—was anxious to avoid unnecessary disruptions and could well have censured and removed him.

We had no idea what motivated the man. Perhaps, because Mummy was obviously so deep in thought, he felt slighted by her lack of attention to his menacing presence. It was unusual for guards to touch people in that way—their usual roll call "touch" was a demeaning slap, warranted or not!

A favorite punishment for misdemeanors was a long kneeling session in front of the commandant, followed by some heavy face slaps. On the whole, unlike unfortunate internees in some other camps, we couldn't really complain about maltreatment in our own particular situation, as long as we kept out of trouble!

Unfortunately, there were a few informers in our midst. A telltale sign for a couple of them was the simple fact that they never lost weight! In Yu Yuen Road, one shunned informer instigated the arrest and one-week detention at Bridge House of an internee who concealed a radio under the floorboards of his room. He returned to camp after his ordeal, visibly battered.

At the end of the war the informers attempted to speedily fade out of sight, but several were apprehended and beaten up by our own people.

Life in the bleak surroundings of broken-down Yangtzepoo camp was extremely depressing. Our years of incarceration had exacted a huge toll on our physical health and mental well-being. There were many new cases of tuberculosis and other serious ailments, and hardly any medical supplies left.

Daddy spent two-and-a-half months in hospital after undergoing surgery for hemorrhoids—they called it *piles*—a condition that plagued him most of his life. Although the nature of his ailment, and everything involved in treating it, was the "butt" of our jokes, we knew he was constantly in a lot of pain.

"One day," he said, "the doctors came and told us Americans planes had sneaked in, missed their intended target and accidently bombed Hongkew, killing several hundred people! The Japanese were very unhappy—they felt their defenses were weak if allied planes could get through their lines."

My father returned from hospital bearing a small amount of precious butter, extracted from his daily milk allowance by vigorously shaking it until the separated butter rose to the top.

Every three months each of us should have received one American Red Cross food parcel. In two-and-a-half years we only received a total of three per head. After the war Japanese warehouses were found stacked with misappropriated Red Cross parcels.

Desperate smokers, given a meager issue of fifty cigarettes per month, experimented unsuccessfully with dried grasses and leaves to find a substitute for tobacco. After coughing and choking from their initial efforts, they settled on dried, used tea leaves as the best of a bad lot, in spite of the foul stench it produced! Strangely, we discovered later that tea smoking was practiced in many POW camps.

Fruit was only issued at Christmas. Sometimes we were given peanuts, which were crushed into a well-disguised imitation of peanut butter.

On a few occasions, during Jewish holidays, we received small food parcels from my maternal grandparents. Mummy loved getting walnuts and almonds. Those free souls on the "outside," wearing armbands marked with an X, had very little comfort and were also struggling to exist throughout the war years. Everything was in short supply and money was scarce. Earning power in most sectors had seriously diminished, forcing people to sell personal goods and valuables so they could buy food and bare necessities. They had to do a lot of under-the-table work—buying and selling on the black market that had thrived from the very start. There was no free trade. The Japanese army and Chinese merchants controlled all big cargo transactions.

The Japanese had appropriated anything of value for the war effort.

Everyone cautiously avoided committing the slightest misdemeanors, or anything that would attract close scrutiny by the occupiers. There were more beggars and thieving urchins than ever before, hanging around, waiting to pounce on frail elderly people and other unsuspecting victims.

By now, news of rapid American advances across the Pacific was filtering through to us. Air raids commenced and continued with such intensity, we thought we would all be blown up! American planes whined overhead, explosions shook the foundations of every building. We all ran for shelter. Remarkably, no one was hit—then or later!

We cheered and waved madly when they flew low over our camp. The end was near—it had to be *very* near!

## LAST DAYS IN CAMP

Early in the morning of August 10, 1945, voices started shouting over the camp fence. "The war is over, THE WAR IS OVER!" The message was immediately relayed to members of the dormitory, internees dumped like garbage in miserable cubicles formed by hung-up bed sheets and curtains. The skeptical answer was, "Oh yeah?"

As more and more excited voices shouted, "The war is over!" the news coming over the wall began to be convincing. "Perhaps it's really true," we said, with the first glimmer of hope.

Later that morning I watched an internee's old mother arrive at the gate with flowers. "My daughter, my darling daughter," she cried, "it is peace—the war is over!" Hediki, one of our "smart aleck" guards, grabbed her roughly by the wrist and dragged her fifty yards through the main gate into the camp. She was dealt one of the last of the numerous face-slappings we had been subjected to in our three years of prison life. Her daughter was called into the guardhouse and underwent half an hour of grueling questioning. We heard the loud cracking sound of her being violently slapped on her face. The old lady was dismissed with a warning not to return to the camp.

That very same evening, headlines in a Japanese newspaper announced:

### JAPAN AGREES TO POTSDAM TERMS

The Potsdam Declaration was a statement issued on July 26, 1945, by Harry S. Truman, Winston Churchill, and Chiang Kai-shek. It defined the terms of surrender for Japan, stating that if Japan did not surrender it would face "prompt and utter destruction."

The news was read out to a stunned audience. "It's true, then—it's true!" Although excitement ran high, everyone was too subdued, tired, and nerve-racked after the long internment to show any wild emotion. Also, the Japanese guards were still around us, threatening, "If you listen to 'false rumors' and became disorderly, Commandant Hashimoto will not hesitate to call in the Japanese Gendarmerie, and will refuse to take any responsibility for their actions!"

During the next few nerve-racking days the guards were getting tough, and swore that no matter what happened in Japan their one million soldiers in China would go on fighting. Levels of anxiety increased dramatically. We were aware of Japanese atrocities to civilians and internees in all parts of Asia, and had a cautiously circulated copy of *Reader's Digest* containing the story of the "Nightmare of Nanking."

Some guards, who were usually friendly and talkative to the children during our long incarceration, suddenly became hostile and sullen. I kept a safe distance after one or two of my attempts to communicate with them were greeted with cold menacing stares. It was frightening, and painfully beyond my childish understanding.

Allied planes had been appearing above. They dropped masses of pamphlets over the Shanghai area. Everyone scrambled to get one of the papers that read:

## ATTENTION ALLIED PRISONERS
ALLIED PRISONERS OF WAR AND CIVILIAN INTERNEES, THESE ARE YOUR ORDERS OR INSTRUCTIONS IN CASE THERE IS A CAPITULATION OF THE JAPANESE FORCES.

1. You are to remain in your camp areas until you receive instructions from this Headquarters.
2. Law and order will be maintained in the camp area.
3. In case of a Japanese surrender there will be allied occupation forces sent into your camp to care for your needs and eventual evacuation to your homes. You must help by remaining in the

area in which we know you are located.

4. Camp leaders are charged with these responsibilities.

5. The end is near. Do not be disheartened, we are thinking of you. Plans are under way to assist you at the earliest possible moment.

A.C. WEDEMEYER
Lt. Gen. U.S.A.
Commanding

On the morning of the 14th of August, Commandant Hashimoto ordered the whole camp in front of A Block for a speech. As usual, the swaggering commandant and his entourage of officers stood on a platform, still believing that elevating themselves would give them stature. His words were taken down in shorthand by one of the inmates:

"On this occasion I shall not greet you or compliment you. I want to give you a warning. Acting on a rumor that the Japanese have been defeated, some of you have been acting in a very arrogant manner towards the guards. I would like to treat you as ladies and gentlemen. Recently somebody took away six bottles of beer and two bottles of sauce. Don't laugh! The room was locked and I suppose the criminal came into the room from the window. And fingerprints were left clearly. In other words I would like to see all you residents in this camp as friends, but now I must change my mind. I cannot keep my words so quiet.

"I should hate some of you residents. Don't smoke please. Of course, I don't care what kind of thinking, and what kind of expectations, and what kind of imaginations you may have, but don't you forget that you are civilian internees, and therefore you should observe regulation and order. I would say, I would not hesitate to take the last measures, if the residents of this camp don't wish to bring these criminals until one o'clock tomorrow afternoon. At least I would like to add a few words, especially for those foolish people who are still thinking and expecting the Americans to come.

"Some of you are so well educated, and such people easily understand that there are more than one million Japanese soldiers in Central China, and this have not had battle at all. Their decision will not change whatever may happen in future. You will remember this. You should realize exactly your position, and you should wait the last chance, which means you should wait the time that you will be exempt. I hope it will be soon. Until that time, I would like to treat all the residents as friends."

The beer episode referred to three young lads, who, thinking the war was truly over, got into the Commandant's quarters during the night and celebrated victory with his beer—leading to the one o'clock ultimatum.

The Commandant's words were later printed in *Camp Chit Chat*, a publication best described in its "Preface" as follows:

*Camp Chit Chat* is a human document of high literary merit, portraying significant aspects of the life in the local concentration camps and displaying at the same time the most admirable quality of internees in its robust humor and good cheer through the most trying and even desperate times.

I am pleased to order through the Voice Publishing Co. Ltd., who have undertaken this publication, copies of *Camp Chit Chat* for distribution to all ex-internee families of the Shanghai area as a gift and as a mark of appreciation for their splendid spirit of endurance and contribution to the common cause of freedom.

This volume, I hope, will serve also as a reminder of our responsibility for safeguarding the peace that we have achieved.

Chien Ta-chun
Mayor
Shanghai, March 5, 1946.

One hour before the expiry of the Japanese ultimatum to us, they themselves were kicked out of camp. The camp representative and our visibly nervous commandant were asked to visit the Swiss Consulate. When they returned at about 11 a.m. the whole camp was once again asked to assemble before Block A. The commandant spoke first. He did not tell us we had won the war or that we were free, and he was leaving the camp. He only told us we were "exempted" from camp life.

And then, they all fled. They simply disappeared!

Our representative informed us of the proceedings at the Swiss Consulate, and told us that from twelve noon we would be free.

Most of the camps in Shanghai then performed the following ceremony:

The national flags of Great Britain, the United States, China, Russia, Holland, Belgium, and Australia, were unearthed from secret hiding places, and our boy-scouts performed the ceremony of slowly raising the flags. As each went up the whole camp sang our national anthems, and "God Bless America."

# HOMECOMING

# HOMECOMING

Our camp officials told us to wait awhile longer before leaving because it was still unsafe to venture beyond the camp boundaries. Gunshots could be heard from time to time. We listened for the drone of Allied planes flying above, and watched with indescribable excitement as they began dropping beautiful, colorful parachutes bearing huge parcels of supplies, many of which fell outside the camp and had to be retrieved after dark because of the many lurking snipers.

Chinese bandits posed an additional danger. Once they found out about our parcel drops, they were always around, watching and waiting to steal the boxes—that sometimes broke open on impact—before we got to them. The enormous cartons contained wonderful items we had been deprived of for so long—chocolates, chewing gum, powdered milk, jam, canned corn beef, sardines, coffee, tea, and various other food items. Clothing, underwear, shoelaces, medical supplies, toiletries and sundry small essentials were also included. Some internees were blissfully satisfied with supplies of cigarettes and matches.

A pile of American comic books mysteriously appeared and quickly did the rounds, passing from hand to hand until they were tattered and torn.

In the field beyond the fence, some huge brown horses, shot and abandoned by the fleeing Japanese, lay dead or dying from their wounds. They lay on their sides, emphasizing their mammoth rumps. Large black flies covered the bodies of beasts that had succumbed. Those still alive were twitching, jerking, neighing and groaning. As if from nowhere, loudly shrieking birds of prey appeared, and circled the skies above the fields of death. The August heat and humidity was unbearable, accelerating the decay and creating a rising stench that was nauseating.

One of the dying horses suddenly seemed to sense me staring at him. His beautiful, pain-filled brown eyes, like darkened pools, appeared to look pleadingly straight into my own staring, horror-stricken eyes. I clutched the wire fence in terror but could not tear myself away.

Alongside many other young and older children, I bore witness to terrible sights and sounds until, mysteriously, the field was cleared during the night, probably by starving Chinese. The same field from whence we collected the wonderful parcels dropped by the Allies. The adults were generally not around to share the horror we had just experienced. They were busy with their usual duties and preparations for our departure for home when the "all clear" signal was finally given.

China, land of great diversity and extremes, never hid its abundance of raw agonies and suffering from us. And yet, their beautiful creative works of art are equally abundantly visible.

By the end of the three years, all our food supplies were used up and all our clothing and shoes had worn out. Most of the time we were barefoot. Whenever possible, people had handed down, or bartered clothing, and everything possible had been recycled to death. Necessity had turned Mummy into an instant "hair-cutter," and she bartered haircuts for jam and other available exchange items. We were all thin and undernourished, and many had suffered from the dreaded dysentery and other debilitating illnesses.

The friendly GIs brought the latest music and dances, and re-introduced joy and hope into our lives. Every day they played *Oh What a Beautiful Morning* and other happy songs on loudspeakers outside some camps. One delightful day Daddy called us to see a movie. "Come on everyone—we're going to see *Meet me in St. Louis*." We ran out quickly to join fellow internees seated on benches in the quadrangle in front of Block A. Soon after they started the movie, starring wonderfully talented Judy Garland and Margaret O'Brien, it began to rain! No one wanted to leave—this was the first movie we were seeing since the war started. So they carried on showing it through a downpour that fortunately didn't last very long.

Once again, our spirits uplifted and restored, we gleefully sang parodies of various songs, including "Whistle While You Work," from *Snow*

*White and the Seven Dwarfs. Our* version differed from several others—some very vulgar—and went like this:

> *Whistle while you work*
> *Mussolini bought a shirt*
> *Hitler wore it,*
> *Churchill tore it*
> *Whistle while you work.*

When it was finally possible, I accompanied Daddy back to see what had happened to our apartment since we left it so long ago. Yangtsepoo camp was further away from our home than Yu Yuen Road had been, so we took a tram for the first part and then walked the remaining short distance through an alley to our home on Nan Yang Road. I was a tiny eight-year-old, and Daddy was a six-foot tall man, who held my hand tightly and took large anxious strides. I had to run to keep up with him! I could sense his mounting apprehension and excitement.

We entered the walled garden of my childhood memories. The magnolia tree was in full bloom and seemed to have grown taller. Large, fallen white petals lay strewn on the ground, shaded by the tree.

We climbed the two flights of steps and entered the apartment. Daddy made a strange sound, and covered his eyes for a moment with a large hand. Almost everything was gone—they had stripped us of all but a few dinner plates, an old table, some iron bedsteads, and a nest of three small tables that had a sticker with Japanese writing on it.

That night we slept on the floor, on old blankets we brought with us. The heat was stifling, so we didn't need any covers. Before going to sleep in our own home, I joined Daddy in prayer, "*Sh'ma Yisrael*. Hear Oh Israel…"

The move back home, in November 1945, was difficult, but exciting, because we were no longer captives. Many others had left before we did. The Red Cross helped return our camp belongings by truck, and gave all British nationals some money for food and other essential expenses. Our home was refurnished with various household items and help from family members, and purchases from reasonably priced auction houses where the valued art of bargaining really paid off.

Daddy heard that a Hongkew refugee with our same surname

claimed we were related and was anxious to meet us. Although our exact relationship with the man was unclear, I accompanied my puzzled father to the dilapidated previous incarceration area for stateless refugees. We walked through the narrow, dirty streets, and found the family living with their tiny baby girl in a small, shabby, sparsely furnished room of a house shared by several families. In spite of these conditions, he and his wife—who smiled a lot and offered me candy and cookies—were happy and grateful to have survived the war.

I busied myself playing with the baby while Daddy and the man spoke, so I never really discovered how he found us and what our connection was—I just understood there was a definite link. Unfortunately, we lost touch when they left Shanghai.

Droves of British and American Navy and military personnel were suddenly visible at every turn, adding a new dimension to the noisiness of the city. They rode in trams, taxis, rickshaws, and pedicabs, and whooped it up, spending money lavishly. Filthy, rag-clad street urchins, hands outstretched, followed them or ran alongside, chanting, *"No mama, no papa, no whisky soda!"* Restaurants and nightclubs blossomed out of nowhere, and post-war euphoria knew no bounds.

The number of both Chinese and Russian prostitutes on street corners spiraled. Pretty "Sing-Song" girls, dark shining hair upswept and secured with fancy combs, wearing jewelry and brightly colored silk cheongsams with long, daringly high slits on one side, vied for the attention of the foreign "big-spenders." Everyone wanted a piece of the cake.

Inflation spun wildly out of control. The black market thrived. Whilst it was still possible, many wealthy Chinese and foreigners with foresight immediately moved their hoarded gold and other assets to Hong Kong.

We got on slowly and resolutely resettling ourselves. Once again we attended services at Ohel Rachel Synagogue and socialized with relatives and friends. By the end of the war approximately 24,000 Jews were still living in Shanghai, but soon the number dwindled as families emigrated abroad.

Daddy reconnected with his pre-war contacts and worked tirelessly to re-establish his business interests. Years later, thirsting for every bit of information about that period, I asked, "So, when you started doing business again you had your own files, and everything—you just had to pick up your connections?"

"When we went back there was nothing to go to," he said. "We just returned, and started to move back in. During that time there was a man in the office—a Viennese refugee—who was with them throughout the war, liaising. He watched, so he knew all along what the Hell was going on. We didn't kick him out, because he was someone who could help us. When the Japanese took over the business *they* paid all the salaries. We found out our old Chinese employee was the 'number one man,' in charge of the warehouse section. He carried on all those years with the Japanese. They didn't kick everybody out—they had to have the key workers there.

"Very slowly, the Chinese came to do business. More cargo came— from America, England, Europe—from everywhere. Coming in from far ports, going out to Europe…"

My father sounded excited as he related long-buried memories of the gathering post-war business momentum in Shanghai. Hearing and watching him, I too felt a surge of undefined, mixed emotions course through me.

"That was your main business, wasn't it? Warehouses—godowns?"

"Yes, and property. I was buying and selling—brokering."

"Property as well! Industrial, commercial, domestic—what was it? As a freelance broker?"

"All kinds—houses, vacant land, development of shops—everything. I was on my own. Alone. Nobody helped me," my father said, with a degree of pride.

"Did you work on fixed commission?"

"I got 2.5% commission if I was direct. If I shared I got one-third of one house. It all depended…" he replied, leaving the sentence in mid-air.

"And you went into shipping afterwards," reminded my mother, who was listening to everything. "At one time you were shipping out goods and all…"

"When were you in shipping? After the war?" I asked.

"No, no! Then we went into packing—packaging."

This was news to me. No end of surprises from my enterprising father!

"Ok—so why did you travel to India during that period?" After the war my father traveled a few times to different destinations, of which I only have a vague knowledge.

"I went there to survey a shipping of oil. I was supposed to be made to—I don't want to say… You know all these things are… Turn this thing off!" my father commanded, pointing to my tape recorder—his unfinished sentences leaving me guessing and mystified to this day.

Undaunted, I pressed on. "During that time, as things improved in

Shanghai, did you think, *well, this is where I'm going to stay. Everything is all right now.* Did you see yourself carrying on life there, hoping everything would be Ok?"

"That was after 1946. Then it started to deteriorate again," my father said sadly, and continued with a simplistic version of events: "We knew Chiang Kai-Shek was getting cold feet, and was trying to govern people. He put up barbwire fences and all kinds of bloody nonsense. The Communists were coming down, closer and closer, into central China, into Chungking in the North. During wartime Mao Tse-Tung and Chiang Kai-Shek were partners, fighting the Japanese together. After the war one became Communist, and the other, Nationalist."

After WWII everyone hoped, with misplaced optimism, that life—as we once knew it—would eventually return to normal. But it was never to be the same again.

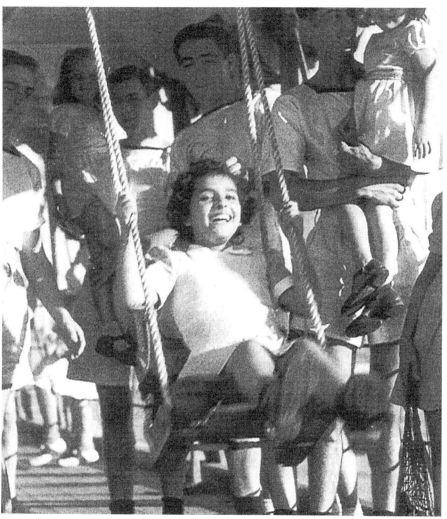

Ester Swinging on HMS Belfast at the tea party in 1945
Photo courtesy of Imperial war Museum, London, UK..

# THE *BELFAST* TEA PARTY—1945

Mummy washed my dark brown hair until it shone, and put a lovely white satin bow on top of my curls.

"Why you look so nice today?" asked Amah. "You velly pletty girl. Gonna mally velly lich man. Makee Mummy and Daddy velly, too much happee."

When alone with us, Amah often chanted her favorite verse and encouraged us to join in with gusto.

> *"Me no savvy, me no care,*
> *Me go mally millionaire.*
> *If he die, me no cly*
> *Me go mally 'nother guy!"*

The invitation, extended by the sailors of the *HMS Belfast*, "cordially invited all ex-internee children to a shipboard party to be held on October 1st, 1945." After the war the ship was in Shanghai doing relief work. It had been out of commission for more than a year due to severe mine damage, and had just recently returned to duty.

Since our release earlier that year from the internment camp, we saw sailors everywhere in the city. They usually walked in groups of two or three and frequently saluted high-ranking officers. Sometimes they staggered drunkenly out of bars and nightclubs, and became rowdy enough to be picked up by vigilant military police who roamed the streets in search of misbehaving personnel.

I could scarcely breathe from excitement in anticipation of the party and kept fidgeting until, exasperated, Mummy threatened to stop helping me to finish dressing. While in Camp, Mummy's friend, Katie Gill, had taught her to design and sew beautifully. With wonderful skill and creativity, Mummy had taken apart Daddy's navy pin-stripe suit and remodeled it into the fashionable outfit she was wearing. Her own pale blue dress had been cut up to make a skirt and top for me. I loved it, and kept admiring myself in the mirror.

We were extremely resourceful and innovative, managing to get by on a very limited budget by making do in countless new ways. It became a challenging game to be the first to come up with good ideas for our survival kit. Mummy frequented crowded markets in narrow back streets, brushing elbows with Chinese shoppers and matching their loudly bargaining voices. She always prepared delicious meals with cheaply priced fresh fish and vegetables.

Daddy was helping to dress Sylvia in a pretty frock, and we were all rushing to be ready in time. I was nearly eight and felt rather "grown up" compared with four-year old Sylvia, but "little girlish" next to David, who would soon be ten. Neatly dressed in white shorts and shirt, he was ready to go, and was impatiently pacing the apartment.

"Will we be able to see the ship's guns and go down into the engine rooms?" he asked insistently. Since the day someone gave him some used toy soldiers and sailors, he immersed himself in endless war games, attempting to re-create all the sounds of bombs whining through skies, air-raid sirens, bullets flying, and crowds screaming.

Amah always covered her ears with her hands. "Aaiee! David—you stop this bad noise. Makee me clazy!"

I inherited my cousin Mona's discarded pee-pee doll, and was forever feeding water down her throat and changing her diapers! I clutched her tightly—she was my only doll. I named her Shirley and tried, as the Chinese do when training their babies, to whistle to make her pee on demand. Chinese babies crouched and relieved themselves through splits in their pants, under their private parts. Amah used to whistle when she wanted us to make a "wee-wee."

"Please, can I take Shirley with me?" I pleaded. "I promise she will be very good—I won't make her pee any more."

"No darling." Mummy's reply was firm. "You'll be so busy eating delicious buns and ice-cream you won't have time to look after Shirley. Maybe you will lose her. You wouldn't like that—would you?" I decided it was a small price to pay and put her to bed.

Mummy looked so glamorous in her new suit. She put on a pretty veiled hat and gloves, and black patent leather shoes that matched her purse.

Finally ready, we all piled into a pedicab and wended our way through streets crowded with trams, rickshaws, bicycles, pedestrians, and vendors. There seemed to be more beggars than ever, hobbling around and frantically tumbling over one another in the hope of getting a little money from the sailors or foreign passersby. Occasionally they would chant a favorite song—"*No Mama, no Papa, no whisky soda!*"

The throng was tightly knitted, and this day, predictably, many obviously ill and diseased people would pass on their ailments.

A crowd of curious observers was at the Bund. They had never seen anything resembling this pageant of excited, well-dressed foreign children and their parents boarding a battleship. The noise at the waterfront was deafening. Ships' foghorns and sirens sounded at sporadic intervals.

"Hey-ho, hey-ho." Coolies chanted in unison as they loaded and unloaded cargo from ships in the harbor.

Waterfront activity had not as yet returned to its busy pre-war days. To those who knew Shanghai, it was generally quieter and more subdued. For newcomers, it still seemed to be the busiest, noisiest, dirtiest, most exciting den of iniquity on earth.

I went up the gangplank holding Mummy's hand. Sylvia held her other hand, and David walked independently. I could hardly contain my excitement—it was wonderful being at the river, even with all the pungent smells that rose from the water. The malodorous scent from the crowded harbor life—of cooking, garbage, fuel spills, mud, body-sweat and refuse—mingled with the smell of cheap soap, from lines of washing waving in the breeze on sampans and junks. It was no less obnoxious than usual, but we welcomed it because we were finally free to smell and breathe the air in locations of our own choice.

It was our first experience of freedom after the internment, which was just like being let out of jail. We had all recently been ill with dysentery and other ailments, brought on by the harsh conditions in camp and lack of basic nourishment. Everyone looked very thin and underfed.

The smiling sailors, in pristine white uniforms, welcomed us warmly onto the deck and made us feel free and loved. They bent down on their knees to be the same height as the children, and kept patting my curly hair, saying, "You're such a pretty little girl." I guess they were missing their own children and families.

Soon, sailors took children from their parents, sat some little ones on their shoulders and played running and racing games. They lifted us up and put smaller children into huge box swings. After waiting awhile for my turn, I was put into a swing they had rigged up, and was swinging high in the air. I couldn't stop giggling and laughing out loud. We were all having a wonderful time. It was obvious the sailors, too, were enjoying themselves immensely.

Beautiful music filled the air as the *Belfast's* own band of musicians played much-loved waltzes, and patriotic and popular melodies of the day. They sang children's songs and sailors danced with little children to the music of *The Teddy Bear's Picnic*. Euphoria reigned supreme.

The smell of the food was intoxicating. We had been deprived of good eating for so long. The tables inside, just off the deck, were laden with cakes, buns, cookies, cheese and crackers, jams, chocolates, sweets, and fruit. The children drank milk and the adults had, to quote Mummy, "wonderful tea." The cooks, overwhelmed by requests for jelly, rushed away to hastily fulfill the orders. Everyone stuffed food into their mouths at high speed, gorging themselves until they literally groaned. A committed few continued to partake of the feast. Unused to large quantities of food, some children suffered for up to two weeks from the effects of their overindulgence. Who could blame them?

Jimmy Corless, one of the tea hosts, chatted with Mummy and taught her to eat cheese and jam together, a delicious and, for us, unfamiliar combination. She invited him to visit our home, and soon he came over, bringing chocolates, cookies, and other delicious treats. The friendship lasted many years through correspondence, and culminated in a visit to Jimmy's family in Newcastle-Upon-Tyne, in England.

We toured the ship and saw how the ship's cats slept in hammocks, as did the sailors! The pampered cats played the important role of eliminating the *Belfast's* unwelcome rat population.

David moved around independently with his friends, and was in seventh heaven when shown the guns. Every now and then he ran to tell us excitedly what he had seen and done. When the sailors were not carrying or playing with Sylvia, Mummy kept a good grip of her hand, while keeping a frantic eye on me as I darted around quickly. She was frightened I would fall overboard!

After several wonderful hours the sailors hugged and helped us all off the ship, blowing kisses and waving us out of sight.

We had all eaten so much it was hard for any of us to move. Also, we didn't want to leave the wonderful sailors of the *HMS Belfast*.

## SHANGHAI BRITISH SCHOOL

The Shanghai British School reopened the doors of its drab stone building when ex-internee teachers were once again able to take up positions. Many had already returned to England, leaving gaps to be filled in by those who could teach different subjects. All our schooling was modeled on the prevailing British education curriculum and system, paving the way for an easy return to England—invariably referred to as "home" by English expatriates, no matter how long they had lived in Shanghai.

Apart from a few Eurasian children from mixed marriages, no purely Chinese children attended the British school. The English population generally frowned upon the mixing of ethnicities.

I was tested for grade suitability because our makeshift camp classes were not adequately structured to place us. The teachers had done a good job and I passed the test sufficiently well to be put into a class one year ahead of my age. I was one of about twenty children, and although I was often bullied because I was smaller than average, and part of a Jewish minority, I managed to hold my own. Often, during school breaks, the children surrounded and taunted me, over and over, with their favorite verse:

*Skinny-bone-banana*
*Had a fatty Amah,*
*Fatty died, Skinny cried,*
*Fatty-bone-banana!*

Thanks to our serious food deprivation during internment, I really was skinny enough after the war for the verse to apply!

At times, the strong overt degree of racism manifested in the British school and other social environments caused me great pain and discomfort. Although I was not yet born at the time, and had no recollection of the event, I was constantly blamed and called to account for the untimely death of Jesus Christ—a tough call for an innocent eight-year-old!

The children often chanted a racially insensitive "song," that caused the starving and long-suffering Chinese great pain, and further stoked the smoldering resentment they felt towards the *Nahkuning*—the foreigners:

> *Chin Chin Chinaman*
> *Velly, velly sad*
> *No money, no food*
> *Velly, velly bad!*

Thanks to all the time spent in the YMCA pool whilst Mummy was practicing diving, my strong competitive swimming ability was in my favor, saving me from torment and gaining me a degree of respect and popularity when I helped my team win races.

My school uniform, a replica of uniforms in England, was a pleated navy blue gymslip and white blouse. Every morning at assembly we said the prayer, "Our Father, which art in Heaven," followed by a hymn. We were all so proud of our British Nationality and sang all the patriotic songs with huge fervor. I swore allegiance to King George, and sang songs of a distant land—that I would first set eyes on twenty years after the war. The same land that would later classify me "not British enough" to receive the *ex-gratia* payment promised to "all who were interned during the war, and British at the time."

I was very excited when I became a Brownie and had a uniform especially made for me by a Chinese tailor. We went to Mummy's favorite lane and ploughed through smothering rows of a bewildering array of colorful, hanging fabrics of every description and texture; silk, lace, satin, velvet, shantung, sharkskin, taffeta, organza, poplin, pique, cotton, tweed, gabardine, pure English wools, and more. I hung on tightly to her hand, fearful of losing her somewhere between the veils! She bargained until satisfied with the price of her choice, and as usual, pre-shrank the material in water before giving it to the tailor.

Most days, we walked three miles to school. One rainy day, Mummy said, "David—you can't walk today. The rain is way too heavy. Here's some money for a rickshaw—just be very careful."

As was usual during downpours, the streets would already be flooded up to two, perhaps even three feet deep in many places. We hailed a passing rickshaw. The scantily dressed, barefoot man was soaked through and dripping water. He lowered the shafts to the ground until the rickshaw lay in a sharply slanted position, enabling us to alight. As David and I clambered onto the tiny landing, the man suddenly lifted the shafts. My foot slipped back and straight downwards off the landing. The large protruding rusty nail, that secured the platform to the shafts, ripped my leg open, and before I knew what happened, I had a long gaping wound in the front of my lower left leg!

Magically, Daddy arrived within moments and sped me away on his bicycle to the doctor, skillfully managing to dodge cycles, vehicles, pedestrians, trams, street vendors, and stray animals. The doctor proceeded immediately, without any available anesthetic, to put seven huge, wide-apart stitches in my wound, while I howled my lungs out.

"Ester must get an anti-tetanus shot immediately if she's to be safe from that dreaded condition," the doctor said. "We don't have any, but if you ask the Navy, you may be able to get it from their supply."

In a strange twist of fate, after multiple calls and footslogging, Daddy was lucky enough to get the serum from the *HMS Belfast*—the very same ship whose crew threw the memorable children's party in 1945!

On the way to school each day, a mile before and after passing an ice-cream factory, the air was full of the aroma of vanilla pods. It was a luxury we could only afford on special occasions. The haunting memory of childhood deprivation led to my life-long love and longing for vanilla ice cream. I resolved to let my own future offspring have it to their hearts' content. Whenever I heard the vendor's bicycle bell ringing outside our home in South Africa, where I lived when married, I never failed to call my kids—"Come on everyone—we're getting an ice cream!"

Imagine my astonishment when, one day, and countless ice creams later, I overheard my younger adult son, Gary, tell a friend, "I hated it when my mother forced us to have an ice cream every time she heard the bell!" Even more enigmatic is the fact that he always loved, and continued, even at age fifty, to love and choose vanilla ice cream over all other flavors!

I was also ecstatic whenever Uncle Jack arrived with a bulging brown paper bag. I knew it contained delicious bananas, a scarce luxury, to name but another sorely missed favorite.

Often, Daddy took us somewhere by bicycle, carrying one child in front and one at the back. He wore bike-clips on the bottom of his pants to prevent them from catching on anything. I loved those exciting rides. Daddy wove his way through sundry crowds and vehicles, sometimes swerving sharply to avoid noisily squawking ducks and chickens, leaving me breathless!

I know he missed his car and always hoped he would find it again somehow, somewhere. He took a tram or bus to work. "It was so dirty," he said, disgusted. "The Chinese used to spit everywhere. Once, I was sitting next to a man who had the window seat. The tram had just been cleaned and the windows were spotless. Then, " Daddy's eyes were twinkling as he continued relating the story, "the man started making throaty noises, getting ready to take aim! He leaned towards me, and I leaned away from him, in unison, wondering where he was going to spit. He repeated this a couple of times, gathering momentum. Suddenly, he flung his head forcefully to the right and spat—ostensibly through an open window, so clean he didn't realize it was closed. He nearly knocked himself out!"

One day, miraculously, Uncle Syddie saw his own car—that had also been impounded by the Japanese—standing at a station. "This is mine," he asserted, and with great excitement, speedily reclaimed it without opposition from a very startled, nervous, and no doubt disappointed, Chinese man. Very few owners recovered their confiscated cars after the war.

In front of many Chinese food stores, flattened roasted ducks were strung up in a row. I imagined them all lying in the middle of the road, waiting to be steamrolled into their flat fate before ascending to "Duckie Heaven!"

Once, after the war, when I was about nine years old, I walked with my little Eurasian girlfriend, Yah-lee, to the Roxy theatre, a few blocks away from home. I was wearing my favorite gorgeous, fluffy, pink angora sweater that I shared with Mummy. Just before our internment she bought it at a sale in the huge Wing On Department Store. The short bolero-style sweater was rather large for me, but I didn't care, and wore it at every opportunity. I had very little more than that one thing I loved.

Whenever possible, we handed down, or shared everything in our small, skimpy family wardrobe. We were really poor, with almost nothing to wear.

The Americans had once again brought all the latest movies to

Shanghai, showing some popular movies repeatedly. We stood in the Roxy foyer, staring longingly at pictures behind glass cases, of Judy Garland in scenes from *The Wizard of Oz.*

A Chinese man approached us. "Would you like to see the movie?" He asked.

"Oh yes," we chirped.

"Fine," he said. "If you give me your sweater, I'll show it to the manager and I'm sure I'll be able to get you in to see the show." Trustingly, I gave it to him and, of course, never saw my sweater again.

# CHINESE NEW YEAR

Amah, David, and I, are fighting our way through the crowded streets surrounding Yu Yuen Road. At times, the thunderous sporadic clap of firecrackers overtakes the deafening din of the excited throng. Today is Chinese New Year, always celebrated in a flamboyant way. It seems as if everyone is out on the streets to view the passing shows and take part in the revelry. If they wait long enough they are certain to see some exciting sideshow, street dancers, or if really lucky, a parade of huge, colorful paper dragons. Many empty little red *cumshaw* packets with gold lettering, the customary gift packets of New Year money, litter the streets.

Walking just ahead of us, I see two men and a woman, obviously foreign tourists, anxious to see as much as possible. Oblivious to any lurking danger, they are chatting excitedly and pointing here and there to something of interest. Following them with increasing closeness, a young Chinese man signals to another young man just to the right of us.

Amah urgently gathers us closer to her and we understand that we are not to acknowledge or interfere in what may be about to happen. My heart is thumping against my ribs, and instinctively, I glance wide-eyed and imploringly at David, not yet ten years old, for protection.

Suddenly, the man close behind the tourists makes his move. He bumps the woman, who cries out in pain as she loses her balance and falls heavily on the cement sidewalk. In the few moments it takes for her male companions to realize she has fallen, the second Chinese man has closed the gap between himself and the foreigners. Deftly, he picks the pocket of the man bending to help his fallen friend rise from the ground. His accomplice has disappeared into the crowd, leaving the foreigners frustrated and confused. There is no way to find the cunning pickpockets who wait for such a golden opportunity.

"Come, we go home now, chop chop," says Amah, pulling us in the opposite direction. "See too much al-leady today." David is tugging Amah's hand. "Aw, come on Amah, just a little longer," David protests. Amah relents and we carry on, fighting our way through teems of people.

I think Amah, in some way, is happy she has seen the pickpockets in action. We have no way of knowing how she really feels about the foreigners, now totaling around fifty thousand in number, who have invaded her land. She never divulges any resentful feelings she may secretly harbor against the multi-ethnic groups that surround her.

Amah is fiercely loyal to us but never speaks about her own immediate family. Sometimes I ask insistently, "Do you have a little girl like me Amah? Do you?" Her face is inscrutable, while her voice drops darkly and dangerously low.

"Why you wanchee know? Too much askee questions! Next time I tell you. Go to bath now!" She dismisses me to some such activity that could easily wait a while longer.

I wonder whether Mummy knows any more than we do about Amah's private life.

More people have filled the streets, and it's becoming impossible to move freely. With each passing moment, the loudness of the excited mass, combined with the ear-deafening din of firecrackers going off in all directions, increases to a crescendo. The Chinese are very proud to have been the discoverers of gunpowder.

David and I clutch Amah's hand tightly, fearful of being separated from her. Terrifying stories abound of kidnapped children who were lost forever to white slavery and prostitution. Some, forced to labor long hours in silk weaving and garment industries, suffered from painful malformed hands. I overheard Mummy and a friend discuss an acquaintance whose young child was last seen being forcibly dragged by her hand alongside the Shanghai railroad tracks.

Nothing of interest escaped our ears, and many a nightmare resulted from these terrifying tales.

"Ai-yaa—ai-yaa!" A woman's scream pierces the air and turns into a wail. A firecracker has injured some unfortunate person, probably a child.

Perhaps, as is common every year during the celebrations, the victim has blown off some fingers, or lost an eye. Most people in the streets can't afford professional medical help and are treated crudely at home. They may purchase some Chinese medicine from the shops, where anything—from powders to snails and snakes—exists in jars lined up on shelves for the world to see.

A performing monkey is drawing a crowd of onlookers when suddenly we hear a gong beating loudly, and a great, excited sound swells up. The paper dragons are coming! The horde makes way for the parade as it arrives in bursts of orange, red, yellow, green, blue and purple. Gigantic, ferocious dragons sway widely from side to side, glass eyes rolling and paper tongues lolling in their swollen heads. Chinese dancers, with heavily accentuated eye makeup, dressed in elaborately sequined, colorful costumes and headgear, accompany them. Some opera singers are with the parade—their highly pitched voices raised in song above the chatter and excited shouts of the massive audience.

Every now and then, at certain points, gong-bearers beat their gongs loudly, emphasizing the dancing and singing.

Now, just ahead of us, I clearly see a new pickpocket with his hand in the back pocket of yet another oblivious foreigner, who is in for a rude shock when he realizes he has been so professionally robbed.

Finally, the huge dragon parade has passed us, and Amah decides we have definitely had enough excitement for the day. Gripping our hands even more tightly she drags us through the throng, cursing and swearing expressively at anyone who blocks her path. She hails a passing rickshaw puller, does her usual bargaining dance, firmly seats us, clambers aboard, and regally waves the bare-footed runner to start the ten-minute journey home.

*8th June, 1946*

T O-DAY, AS WE CELEBRATE VICTORY,

I send this personal message to you and all other boys and girls at school. For you have shared in the hardships and dangers of a total war and you have shared no less in the triumph of the Allied Nations.

I know you will always feel proud to belong to a country which was capable of such supreme effort; proud, too, of parents and elder brothers and sisters who by their courage, endurance and enterprise brought victory. May these qualities be yours as you grow up and join in the common effort to establish among the nations of the world unity and peace.

Top: Welcoming letter received from King George by Hazel Minny and ex-internees in England.

Bottom: Armband worn by Hazel Minny, Weihsien camp, Tientsin.

# THE MINNY FAMILY

In 1947, after spending two years in England, my father's sister, Leah Minny, returned to Shanghai with her four children, and mother-in-law. It was wonderful seeing them. We shared accommodating them, with her sister Sally, who was still our neighbor. My older cousins Hazel and Ed, and their grandmother, stayed with us.

The Minnys lived in Tientsin before the war and were interned there—at Weihsien.

Sixty-two years later, during a visit to Sydney, Australia, where most of my father's family made their home after the war, I gleaned much information I could never have assimilated when I was ten years old. We spent hours sharing stories and comparing our pre-war lifestyles and experiences as Japanese POWs.

"In Tientsin we mixed mainly with English people," Hazel said. "We were close to the Gobi Desert—our house had a double set of windows so the dust would be trapped between them and not come into the house.

"After Pearl Harbor, and before our internment, we were confined to the British Concession. Our school was taken over by the Japanese so we had lessons in peoples' homes. Everyone over the age of ten was compelled to wear a red armband with a Japanese character meaning 'British.' My number was 5 55. My father had a copy of the armband painted on our black wrought iron front gate, as a reminder to wear it."

This contrasted with Shanghai, where—as far as I knew—children did not wear degrading red armbands emblazoned with the bold black letter 'B.'

"One year," Hazel said, "there was a flood, and we had to travel around by sampan rowed by our servant. My father was shipped to work, and our doctor paid house visits the same way when anyone was sick. Our house had a basement, two floors, and an attic, and the water came up to the first floor above the basement—where our servants lived. The kitchen was there too, so it all had to be moved up one floor. The water came up to the wall of our house—we had to walk on top of the wall to get inside!

"Wow!" I said. "I'm envious. I wish our floods were as exciting as yours. Ours were just good to slosh about in. Knee deep."

"As in all camps," continued Hazel, "we had roll calls outside our rooms every day. But after two men escaped we all had to assemble in a field.

"My mother used to buy food over the wall—from the Chinese outside the camp. On one occasion my father asked me to check if she was all right. I went to the wall and asked my mom to give me her purchases. She said, 'Be quiet and go home!' I was about eleven... When I persisted, she gave me the bundle and, as only a child would, I walked straight past the guardhouse on my way to our room. The most officious Japanese officer came out. 'What are you carrying?' he asked. Thinking quickly, I said, 'I don't know—somebody gave it to me.' He escorted me to the guardhouse and notified my parents, who came to rescue me. Luckily, we had civilian Japanese in charge of us—they allowed us to take the food and go.

"We had a pram—the guard wanted it for his wife. My mother told him she was expecting a baby and would need it, so he didn't take it from us."

I pondered this information. The barbaric, bestial cruelty of the Japanese was well known and documented. We were lucky to have been spared the fate of some allied internees in other camps in Asia, and to have escaped the wholesale slaughter suffered by Chinese victims in Nanking, and elsewhere in China.

"Mom always told us that someday a train would come and take us home," Hazel said, "so my sister June, who was only four, went out the camp gate with a little boy to wait for the train—the guards allowed them to do so! When we couldn't find her, we were all worried that she, like another little boy, had fallen into a cesspool used for vegetable waste—earning him the nickname *Daniel the Cesspool Diver*. Fortunately it was not night soil!

"There was a tunnel in the grounds of the hospital—the children often went through it. It was only earth held up by a few beams, and could have collapsed and buried us at any moment! I'm sure our parents never knew about this."

*How similar we all were*, I thought, recalling how I rescued David after he fell into the cesspool at Yangtzepoo. *If our parents knew half of what we were up to in camp*....

"A lot of Nuns and Fathers were interned with us," Hazel said. "Sister Blander created a stage-play—*The Magic Toyshop*, and occupied children during summer vacation. Miss Aterbury—an artist—taught us to draw. Both were American."

"Yes," I said, "We, too, had our share of dedicated teachers and gifted individuals who helped us get through the difficult internment years. I don't remember complaining of boredom!"

Hazel said, "At the end of the war seven Americans parachuted into our camp. We used their parachute material to decorate a field, which the next lot of American planes mistook as marking the site for dropping food parcels—instead of outside the camp boundary. Tins and boxes came flying everywhere! I was outside, and decided to check on my mom and baby brother in our room. As I made my way, I saw a large tin from one of the parcels falling right near me, so I ran with several others into a nearby toilet area for shelter!

"We lived in Block 39, which had six rooms. There was a compound behind us, and a larger building that the Americans occupied. Every morning, over loud speakers, they blasted out the song, *Oh What a Beautiful Morning*.

"We walked to Weihsien town—quite an experience after being incarcerated for so long. I went with a friend for a long walk outside our camp without telling anyone. We enjoyed the walk, but got into a lot of trouble when we returned. Anything could have happened to us—we were too young to realize the danger...

"We were supposed to return to Tientsin by train, but the Chinese Nationalists, afraid the Communists would attack them after we left, kept smashing the railway! The Americans got fed up with that and flew us back to Tientsin by C47 army planes."

The Minnys waited about two months for the ship that was to evacuate them, and most other internees, to England. They had to keep checking for its arrival at the Tientsin Club.

"During that time I went for walks with my friend, June," Hazel said. "One day she started talking with a Marine on duty outside the American barracks. He began visiting our house and invited us out for a meal. June told him I didn't eat pork, so he ordered us *each* ten fried eggs and fried chicken! We also got friendly with two Marines who supplied us with necessities. They, too, spent a lot of time in our house—they were dying to get home, and invited us to live with them in Ohio. My mother took them shopping for materials for their wives—she knew the Chinese would charge much higher prices if they went alone!

"In December 1945 our evacuation ship, the *Highland Chieftain,* finally arrived. The first port of call was Shanghai. That's when we met all our relatives for the first time since I was two years old," Hazel concluded.

# THE COMMUNISTS

The ominous clouds of communism began to gather. Everyone was talking about the warring Chinese political parties and their advances into new territories. Foreigners were leaving in droves and England began to repatriate her own nationals. Britain, manifesting racial discrimination on a large unforgivable scale, denied passage to most people in our position on grounds we were not originally from England.

The same discrimination prevailed when Daddy was unable to secure passage to any of the Allied countries. Suddenly, the Australian quota was too full, and Canada, quite aware of our lack of finances, wanted an immigration payment of $10,000.

Outside our kitchen door, at the back of our building, the rickety, wooden fire-escape staircase overlooked a Chinese school. Daily, I stood and watched children of all ages being drilled in communistic doctrine. They marched and chanted as one, raised their arms in perfect army-like unison, and sang militant-sounding songs with enthusiasm.

"Ester," Mummy always called, "come back inside! It's too dangerous to stand on the staircase—you could very easily fall."

It was true—when I looked down between the narrow steps, I could see rotten wood and gaping cracks in the flight just beneath our landing. There were patches of old green paint that once, in better days, covered the entire surface. My smallest steps triggered loud creaks! I never ventured any further down the staircase. It was hard to tear myself away, so I dragged out my observation until I knew, by the frantic note in her voice saying, "Ester, come back in NOW!" that Mummy had reached the end of her tether.

Amah took over when Mummy was out playing tennis and volley-ball, or doing one of many other things that filled her days. "Ester! You commee insidee chop chop. Too dangelous. I tellee Mummy if you no listen NOW!"

I don't know whether the children saw me watching them. They seemed completely caught up in their fervor and commitment to the party. The take-over had begun. Communism, no longer a fledgling movement, had become a frightening force to be reckoned with.

Daddy's family had started leaving Shanghai. We went to the warehouse where our grandmother stored all her beautiful possessions. I saw the Blackwood furniture, the impressive grand piano, multi-sized decorative ceramic ornaments, intricately carved trunks and many other items—soon to be lost forever, when the iron curtain finally dropped. I opened the piano and touched the keys lovingly for a while, striking a couple of notes softly, before being gently but firmly pulled away. The ivory keys disappeared as the lid went down. I felt suddenly cold in the dimly lit warehouse.

In flashes of memory, I remembered the piano in a different setting, and heard the ghostly sounds of it being played by Daddy and his musically talented family.

Most of the expansive warehouse was jam-packed to the ceiling. It smelt strongly of rat-droppings, visible everywhere. Most people kept pet cats at home to control the explosion of vermin. Now—frighteningly—rodents, roaches, and spiders, had a blissfully free run of warehouses and neglected buildings!

I wondered to what extent, during the war, the starving Chinese were responsible for the diminished cat population, and knew with horrified certainty that dog-meat was not off-limits! At crowded smelly markets, they haggled loudly over cute meowing kittens that crawled and tumbled over each other, frantically clawing the mesh of their small cages that were strung up in rows. I heard how, after slaughtering them by boiling, excoriation, and other unmentionably inhumane methods, cooks covered animal delicacies with wonderful, tasty sauces. It seemed anything that had four legs was fair game!

Chinese stores with entire walls of small, glass-fronted cubicles housing snakes, lizards, scorpions, crickets, centipedes, cockroaches and other creeping, slithering creatures abounded. The Chinese purchased various cage inhabitants for medical, as well as culinary purposes, and crickets, grasshoppers and other choices to keep as pets. It was both thrilling and scary to step into one of those shops.

The warehouse visit seemed to sadden everyone. It emphasized the pending departure and inevitable division of families. Daddy was a young man, only thirty-eight years old, and Mummy, barely thirty-one. They had already experienced the bitterness of forced, extended separation during the war.

I felt their pain, and began to develop what would become a lifelong feeling of protectiveness towards them. Wanting to shelter them, I no longer shared my every fear and failure. Inevitably, I developed a self-reliant inner strength, prematurely and abruptly signaling the end of my childhood.

A new introspective attitude developed and conversations took a different turn—from false hope to a new realistic awareness.

"Let's go! It's time to leave," my father said.

In the autumn of 1947, when I was nine years old, my parents, sadly resigned to the inevitable, decided to relocate to Hong Kong. Daddy left first, in October, hoping to re-establish his once-thriving business on the British-controlled Island. In his letters he described it as *Paradise made of cotton wool*. We followed about three months later, to be in time for the start of the new school year. It was still winter and the weather was freezing cold.

We left in the nick of time. Many waited too long and had great difficulty getting out when the Communists took control of Shanghai on May 27, 1949, and shut all the gates.


Boarding the huge ship for the three-day journey that took us to our new home was exciting, particularly for the children. We didn't fully comprehend the pain of the departing adult Shanghailanders, many of whom were born, or had spent a lifetime, in China.

Putting on a brave face, a few people were singing various nostalgic songs of farewell, including Harry Parr-Davies' well-known song, written in 1939—*Wish me luck, as you wave me goodbye.*

Everyone stood at the rails, wistfully watching the majestic skyline of the Bund slowly diminish, until it finally disappeared into my distant childhood memories. I was overwhelmed with a tremendous sense of loss…

Then, I turned to watch and wait about two hours for the muddy Whampu and Yangtze Rivers to meet the Pacific Ocean.

"Look! Look!" Excited voices were raised and hands pointed. There it was—the distinct line dividing the murky brown water from the brilliant blue ocean that seemed to stretch into infinity.

It was *my* new infinity, carrying with it the promise of future untold adventures of my life. The crashing waves echoed the voices of those around me—"*Zai hui*—goodbye Shanghai. Goodbye."

# HONG KONG

BENJAMIN FAMILY 1951

Ester            David          Sylvia

     Liza                 Benjy

# HONG KONG

My father arrived in Hong Kong, the "Fragrant Harbor," on October 21, 1947. He stayed with my aunt Victoria's family in a large, elegant home on Conduit Road, some distance up-mountain on the island. As planned, the rest of us arrived before commencement of the 1948 school year, shortly after my tenth birthday.

I had bid an emotional, fond "farewell" to my early childhood days in Shanghai...

Daddy joined his brother Syddie in a new business he had launched—as Hong Kong agents representing *Associated Generale*, a big Swiss company. He rented a small room and employed two or three Chinese and Cantonese staff. They also re-employed Mr. Yip, the same Cantonese Comprador who worked for them in Shanghai.

"It was the Controller's company," my father said. "We were the quantity and quality surveyors—looking after their business, and so on... We sent someone to check the quality of all cargo that came in. If it was good we said, 'We'll pass this.' If we didn't say 'Pass,' it didn't go—they wouldn't send anything that was rotten!"

"What was it?" I asked. "Rice?"

"Any cargo—anything. It all went to the laboratory, and if it came out with a good report, it was attached... We surveyed cargo for people who were shipping out. The overseas buyers stipulated that it *had* to be supervised by *Associated Generale* people in Hong Kong. They said, 'Please examine the cargo you're shipping, and ensure that it's good.' Peanuts, oil, rice, agar-agar, and more—we graded everything—good, bad, or average quality. We delivered our report and documents to the bank. They said, 'Ok—good cargo,' and paid us; the cargo went on board and was shipped to its destination."

My grandmother, Essie, was also there.

"And much did the old woman care whether I was her son," my father said bitterly. "They must have thought, *call your brother—he's the only one you can rely on.* So Syddie sent me a telegram: *Offer you the job, $1500. a month. If you accept you must also work in the office on Saturdays, and so on…* What kind of job? I never got fifteen pennies from him!" my father stated, still rankling from the injustice he suffered so long ago. "I didn't want to go—I didn't want to go!" he repeated mournfully. "Maybe that's why I had so much bad luck in my life…" My father, always observant, never worked on the Sabbath.

"Then," he continued, pointing at my mother, "*She* said, 'you can't throw away a thing like that—let's go to Hong Kong.' She was so happy— her sister, Victoria, was there.

"I carried on in Hong Kong, thinking, *it's going to be good.* Then I saw it was *really* all *Paradise made of cotton wool.* It never changed. After a month, I couldn't get my salary—no salary and no money! I don't know how the hell they made arrangements! They took money from me, and paid me back, and took money… I had to take between $300 and $600 home for us to live on. It was very bad—altogether a black time!"

"So it wasn't because of the Communists that you left Shanghai," I said, with new insight.

"No! I was fed up with Shanghai—finished with it!" My father said, vehemently. "What was Shanghai? Finished!" he repeated, for emphasis, in case I missed the message. "It was going to the Communists—everybody knew…

"Your mother knew very well she had to follow soon after I left, so she sold our flat to Tommy Johnson's sister for $2000. She sent the money to some Chinese bank in Hong Kong—and I got it!"


Our first home was an apartment on Granville Road, very close to Nathan Road, a main artery in Tsim Sha Tsui, Kowloon, the Chinese translation of *Nine Dragons.* It was a bustling, sub-economic area, mainly populated by Chinese—about twenty minutes walk to the Star Ferry terminal, where ferries constantly conveyed masses of passengers to and from the island. It was a new, and immensely pleasurable experience for me. I eavesdropped on Chinese from different parts of China conversing in Pidgin English. They all looked alike, but spoke different dialects. "Seventy-two," my father always told us with conviction, "and none the same!"

I've been unable to positively confirm this figure, and wondered where he got his information. Although only between seven to eleven dialects are generally recognized as the major ones, there are, indeed, an almost unlimited number, all differing sufficiently to render them nearly impossible for Chinese of different dialects to understand each other. Nonetheless, they can communicate in writing—because the written word is the same.

Sometimes, as droves of people, packed like sardines, disembarked from ferries or trams, I saw pickpockets in action. They rifled the back pockets of unsuspecting victims, and speedily slipped away through the crowds. This was reminiscent of what I often witnessed in Shanghai—and seemed endemic. Signs were posted everywhere warning people to *BEWARE OF PICKPOCKETS!*

Our Chinese building owner ran a general dealership store at street level and his family had a penthouse apartment, directly above us. He always greeted us cordially and invited us over now and then. We spent a lot of time in his store. On Chinese New Year he gave us a few coins in red *cumshaw* packets, and some sweet and salty *tuck*. We lit cheap strings of firecrackers and played games downstairs with neighboring Chinese children. It didn't take us long to learn Cantonese.

One day while bathing I looked up suddenly and saw the owner's scrawny teenage son, Ah Wah, spying on me through a gap he created by removing one of the thin, slatted-glass windowpanes above the bathtub. He was standing on an extremely rusty, protective iron grid that was level with the top of the window. Our apartment windows flanked three sides of a large square empty space that ran all the way from top to bottom of the building. I caught a fleeting glimpse of his frightened eyes before he bounded upwards at high speed and disappeared without a trace! Anyone weighing a few more pounds than Ah Wah would have broken through the grid and plummeted to certain death!

Years later I found out my mother also caught him spying on her!

We often took The Star Ferry to visit Aunt Victoria, and spent most Saturdays and Jewish holidays with her family. She picked us up at the terminal and drove home in her Austin, expertly maneuvering narrow, winding, uphill roads. After Shanghai's flat terrain, the view of the mountains and harbor was breathtaking! We always walked quite a mountainous distance, huffing and puffing, to Ohel Leah Synagogue to attend services, and returned home to feast on a banquet of delicious food prepared by two expert cooks—my mother and her sister. The extra-long table, that extended to seat thirty-six people, groaned with platters of curry, mountains of raisin-dotted, yellow saffron rice, chicken and beef dishes, Chinese food, Japanese Sukiyaki, and other delicacies too numerous to mention.

Soon after our arrival in Hong Kong David celebrated his Bar Mitzvah at Ohel Leah, and the ceremony was followed by a scrumptious reception at Aunt Victoria's house. Some of our Shanghai friends, also living in the Colony, were invited and were overjoyed to re-unite and reminisce with everyone.

# KING GEORGE V SCHOOL

King George V School, Hong Kong. Photo courtesy of Meghan Spillane, Community Development Manager, KGV.

The day finally arrived for us to register at CBS—the Central British School. It was January, after the long winter school break. The weather was much milder than the freezing winters we experienced in Shanghai. I was really excited! My father took David and me on a double-decker bus to the school, at the top of a hill. After leaving the busy main road, two sharp uphill right turns and one left turn brought us to the school buildings.

After the end of the war the school was used as a military hospital, and British doctors lived there. In the Hall's main entrance, the words *Never in the Field of Human Conflict* were inscribed, in reference to Winston Churchill's memorable speech to Parliament on August 20th 1940, when he said, "Never in the field of human conflict was so much owed by so many to so few."

I knew some of the many children waiting to be interviewed. They had been in my camp and school in Shanghai. I skipped a class after the war, and now, because of our unconventional camp schooling, we would all be tested again for correct class placement.

The broken continuity of education, and widely differing curriculum in various countries during the war years, had reportedly resulted in pupils being one to one-and-a-half times below pre-war standards.

When it was my turn I was ushered into a classroom and seated opposite a kindly male teacher. He put me at ease by first asking a few questions about our life in Shanghai before asking, "Can you spell *house?*"

"Yes," I answered—relieved the question was so easy. I proceeded with conviction to spell my friend Magda's surname—"H-a-a-s."

"No, my dear—that's completely incorrect," he said, looking surprised. "That's not how you spell *house.*"

"I thought you asked for my friend Magda Haas' name," I said, filled with disappointment and verging on tears. How could I have made such a stupid mistake—and so completely misunderstood him?

"Never mind," he said kindly. "Let's try again, shall we?"

"It's spelled 'h-o-u-s-e,'" I corrected myself with great relief.

He tested my general knowledge with a few questions and then selected a few more words that I managed to spell with ease. I passed with flying colors and skipped a class again! Now I was two years younger than average age—the portent of a very difficult time ahead for me. Snobbish British classmates, taking advantage of my petite build and age, taunted and bullied me endlessly. During breaks I was surrounded and poked with rulers and sharp pencils, and generally ostracized. I was seldom invited to their birthday parties. Once again, I was regularly being accused of killing Jesus, and being called to account on behalf of all Jews for the heinous crime I had committed some two thousand years ago! There were very few Jewish children at the school.

A small number of lovely girls befriended, and sometimes even bravely defended, me. With particular fondness I remember Suzanne Hewson and Jeanette Dobson. I never saw them again after we left China. There were others, but their names, regretfully, have slipped my memory. I could never forget Susan, a perpetrator who delighted in my misery, and another Jewish classmate, who, fearing what I endured, ingratiated herself by participating wholeheartedly in "ganging-up" on me. Using my name she made rude calls to classmates' homes, resulting in Susan's mother's written request to *remove my daughter from her unsuitable seat next to Ester Benjamin*. Mrs. Hill, our wonderful class teacher, found out, and publicly denounced the "despicable calls."

During school exams kids jockeyed to sit near me so they could ask me for answers—especially during French and math tests. That's when I was always in demand!

Mary Riddle, the brightest child in our class, was a Eurasian with an English father and Chinese mother. We were always competing for marks. I don't recall ever seeing her smile—she was very reserved and the children usually left her alone. I think they were in awe of her ability. She only participated in compulsory sporting activities and physical training.

There were three school *Houses* that competed against each other, and also against many different schools. David and I were assigned to "Nightingale House"—winner of the most sports trophies. The other two Houses were "Upsdell" and "School," renamed "Rowell" in 1950.

Because I held my own in sports events I was regularly included in the swimming and field hockey teams, usually playing center half. The minute the bell rang for break I would charge down to play on the huge sunk-in field that easily accommodated two games simultaneously. I often saw David, who also loved sports, playing cricket or football on the adjacent field. Whenever possible, we both stayed after school hours to participate in games.

During the occupation the Japanese had used the school as a hospital, and it was rumored bodies were buried under the sports field. As well, the pavilion at the bottom of the field was said to have been a torture chamber during the war, and many strongly believed it was haunted.

David didn't seem to have serious racially motivated difficulties, and did better socially. But his schoolwork suffered because he was really lazy—he shirked homework, failed a class, and stayed down in the "B" stream. His marks were so bad, Mummy, who could never bear to inflict any pain on David, broke a flimsy Chinese umbrella on him, and then, disgusted, threw it out the fourth-floor window! Luckily it never hit any passersby! David thought it rather funny, and didn't work any harder at his schoolwork. He stayed in the "B" stream until we left Hong Kong.

My father never seemed to play a part in monitoring our school progress—probably because my mother, fearing his punishment would be too severe, kept our report details to herself. My father was wont to lash out fairly uncontrollably at times.

As an adult, my brother—surprising us all—passed many more exams than school ever demanded of him, and achieved substantial success in the business world.

Every morning we stood in rows in the assembly hall and recited The Lord's Prayer. With raised voices we sang the song that was both the school's motto and anthem:

*Here we are gathered from many a nation,*
*Arts to acquire that our peoples may serve.*
*Characters moulded by strict regulation*
*Honour demands we this motto observe:*
*Honestas Ante Honores, honesty first then glories*
*Loud raise the echoing chorus, Honestas Ante Honores.*
*Bold as the Lion Crest, blazoned on every breast*
*Loud let resound the chorus, Honestas Ante Honores.*

Dr. Graham Cumming, father of two King George V (KGV) schoolgirls, composed the words, and Mrs. Simpson, our music teacher, composed the music. We sang many patriotic, and "olde" English songs in her class. She recruited me into the school choir and put me in the center dividing line—because I had such a loud voice and could keep my side on track! Some kids complained, and asked me to "shut up!"

After the war everyone exhibited great patriotism and pride in the achievement of the Allies.

On April 30th 1948, Sir Alexander Grantham, governor of Hong Kong, and his wife, Lady Grantham, presiding over the school prize giving, began his speech by praising us for being distinguished in Hong Kong for our good manners and politeness. Then, saving a huge surprise for the conclusion of his speech, he announced that we would no longer be called Central British School—it was the King's pleasure that the school be renamed after his illustrious father, King George V.

The hall erupted in cheers and loud clapping—we were all so honored! Never was our anthem, *Honestas Ante Honores*, sung with such gusto as it was after the Governor's proclamation!

Some teachers from Shanghai were also at the school—in particular I remember our sports teacher, Billy Tingle, who, many years before, had also been my father's instructor. He was very fond of me because I was a strong swimmer and passionately keen on sports. Once, during unexpectedly freezing weather, I was the only one who swam in the gala—diving into the icy water and swimming every race in the huge, indoor pool, with no competition! I caught a severe cold and spent several days in bed. Mr. Tingle called my parents to tell them he thought I was the bravest kid in the school.

Ester as Girl Guide Patrol Leader. Second from the right, in the back row.

David became a Boy Scout, and I joined the Girl Guides and took the oath:

*I promise that I will do my best:*
*To love my God,*
*To serve the Queen and my country,*
*To help other people*
*And to keep the Guide Law.*

We took it all very seriously. I passed some skills-tests and proudly sewed the badges I acquired onto the sleeves of my blue uniform—that I've kept to this day! I was the daughter of an inspired Guide Leader, and had heard all the songs we sang at meetings since I was a little child.

# NEW BEGINNINGS

Now that I was a little older, I was observing things differently than I had in Shanghai, and really enjoying everything Hong Kong offered, free, or at low cost. We had endless fun on organized launch trips, sometimes swimming in the middle of the ocean. We visited many bays and beaches on the long, twisting and turning coastline. Sheltered by mountains, the bays seldom had large waves, making swimming extremely pleasurable.

Repulse Bay, on the island, was a very popular beach for us all. We bused there regularly and spent hours picnicking, sunbathing, and swimming out to the buoy, a little distance from the beach, where we could dive and swim around in deep water. There are different theories as to how the bay got its name; one held that pirates—a menace to merchant ships trading with China—used it as a base and were eventually repulsed by the British Fleet. Another, that it was named after *HMS Repulse,* once stationed there. It was developed into a beach in the 1910s, and later, in 1920, the imposing Repulse Bay Hotel was built.

On the ascending road to the New Territories and Canton, on the mainland, there were several beaches with different names denoting the number of miles from a certain point. At a famous one, and also my favorite—*Silverstrand*, in Clear Water Bay—we had to descend quite a lengthy stairway to reach the water, in which, standing, I could see my feet. At night, and uniquely at Silverstrand, when splashes disturbed uneven surfaces in the water, plankton, in "emergency" mode, emitted a shining, fluorescent, silver-blue colored light!

Sometimes the Guides took us there for a picnic. On one occasion the current was very strong, and before I realized what was happening I was slowly being dragged further and further from the beach! I struggled to return to the group. They hadn't even noticed my slow, out-bound journey!

On some weekends my mother decided we would hike through, and "explore" the beautiful woody areas of the New Territories. Intermittently, we came across deep, smallish, fresh-water mountain pools, and swam in the deliciously cool water. My father couldn't swim, but always floated blissfully on his back. He was enjoying one of these sessions when he suddenly lost his balance, panicked, and was going down. He was in real trouble! He fought my mother's efforts to save him, terrifying us, until he finally gave in and allowed her to pull him to safety! Thank goodness she was such a powerful swimmer.

Sometimes we caught buses to Luna Park, or Lai Chi Kok's huge, newly built entertainment center, and enjoyed rides and games. We had very little money, but thankfully, Mummy, always innovative, discovered many sources of affordable enjoyment.

Now and then, with mostly Asian passengers, we took a two-hour ferry to mountainous Lantau, the largest island in Hong Kong, and nearly double the size of the latter. Lantau Peak is almost twice the height of Hong Kong's Victoria Peak. Originally the site of somnolent fishing villages, it was once also a base for smugglers and pirates. During the war, Lantau's tough Chinese resistance movement shifted supplies, and persevered with organized ambushes until the Japanese were defeated in 1945.

The launch trip, walking around the Chinese market, and visiting the fishing sites and beaches, were all exhilarating and exciting events for me. In those years the island was largely undeveloped and under-inhabited, but grew in later years to be home to a large population of inhabitants of diverse nationalities.

One of my school-friends lived on Stonecutters Island, a British Naval and Military base, named when the British used it for quarrying. There were many poisonous snakes on the island, including brown cobra and bamboo snakes. When the Japanese, following heavy shelling, captured the island in December 1941, besides using it for radio transmissions and communications, they housed a snake farm and milked venom to provide antidotes for their soldiers in the Pacific.

I loved being invited to my friend's home to spend the night on the island. We left straight from school and caught the military launch to get there. We pretended it was a secret, fantasy island with pirates, as indeed, there had been in bygone days! The island was not heavily populated yet, so we felt like explorers, collecting bits of pottery and pretty shells.

For a small fee, David and I periodically rented bikes and rode long distances on Kowloon's roads, and through fields and valleys. Once, in an isolated field, we encountered some naked Chinese laborers a short distance away from us. They started laughing and jeering, and waved their private parts at us. It was frightening and dangerous. We sped away and never returned to the site!

I used to wander into stores on the main road leading to the Star Ferry. One day I ventured into a Chinese auction shop. It was jam-packed with sundry, smelly, dilapidated goods. I spotted an old ramshackle bicycle standing amongst a whole pile of dusty furniture. I ran home and told my mother. I begged her to buy it, so we went to the Chinese auctioneer and she bargained with him until they agreed on a price, and the bike was mine. Or so I thought… until David commandeered it. He fixed it up and took over, hardly allowing me to ride my bike.

Once, when I had the bicycle, I rode it down the sharp L-shaped school incline and the brakes failed! I was really lucky to stay alive as I merged, breathless, with the crazy traffic on the main road—buses, cars, rickshaws, pedicabs and more!

One day while riding in front of the school, I swerved to avoid some chickens running across my path. I fell off and broke my leg. My brother was at a scout meeting, so he and his friends practiced their boy-scout skills on me and made a splint—before calling an ambulance that got me to hospital! My leg was encased in a huge plaster and I remained in hospital for several days. I couldn't go to school for weeks, but when I did I was almost a celebrity! Everyone signed my plaster and I kept it for a long time, reluctantly giving it up when we left Hong Kong.

David had the bike all to himself for a long while after my accident.

In 1957, when I revisited Hong Kong, I was invited to address the school children. I told them the story of my mishap. They laughed their heads off! Bike riding was no longer allowed in front of the school.

I missed the piano so much while I was convalescing. When I was able to play it again I supported my leg on a chair and cried while playing all my favorite pieces.

# GROWING UP

The whipped-up wind whistled and howled frighteningly—typhoon! Everyone ran around, frantically closing doors and securing windows that shook, flapped, and banged against outside walls, sending shattered glass shards flying in all directions. Within minutes streets were emptied as people sought shelter from the storm's fury in doorways, stores, and wherever else they found it.

After the lashing rain, when the typhoon was finally spent, the air smelled clean and fresh and the prevailing calm made me wonder whether it was all a dream.

In the aftermath of WWII, the British Colony was flooded with thousands of refugees fleeing Mainland China, greatly swelling the population, and straining resources. By 1949, soon after our own arrival, there were some 300,000 Chinese squatters living in abject squalor, in crudely developed shantytowns on steep hillsides. Flimsy, makeshift shacks were constructed from wood, sheets of corrugated iron, scavenged doors and windows, and other found, useable material. Similar dwellings were also erected on some rooftops.

During typhoons and heavy downpours, hundreds of squatters died from ensuing landslides that relentlessly collected and destroyed everything possible in their downhill rush. Fires also regularly claimed many lives.

The squatters' plight, particularly following catastrophic occurrences, was widely debated, written about, and discussed. But those more fortunate continued to live their complacent lives.

Narrow, concrete-lined *nullahs*—Hindi word for dry riverbeds or ravines—specially designed to prevent flooding of urban coastal areas, were ubiquitous in Hong Kong. During heavy rainstorms, torrents from higher ground rushed down the steep channels and disappeared into reservoirs.

Aunt Victoria's husband, David, was once caught in a storm immediately after leaving a house party. He drove downhill on the steep driveway and failed to take a left turn at the exit. Before he knew what happened, he lost control of his car, skidded off the road and rolled over several times. Remarkably, the vehicle landed on its roof, bridging the *nullah* directly across the road from the house he had just left! His large consumption of alcohol apparently numbed his pain, and he managed somehow to crawl out of the vehicle and return to the party.

An ambulance rushed him to hospital where he was diagnosed with a broken back, and fitted, from the neck down, with a huge cumbersome plaster cast. He was in agony, and remained hospitalized for four months. The cast was finally removed a long while after he was released, and retained as a souvenir and reminder of his narrow escape from death! I couldn't imagine how he actually survived the accident, and the subsequent encasement during the long, humid summer, in such a heavy contraption.

Surprisingly, he pulled through the ordeal extremely well, made a full recovery, and continued for many years to drive a car *and* ride a Harley Davidson motorbike on mountainous roads!


Daddy came home every day for *tiffin*, the lunchtime meal. "It's so bloody hot!" He grumbled, as he removed his jacket and tie. Mummy, braving the heat and humidity, played tennis almost daily at the Kowloon Country Club, KCC, and also regularly practiced her fancy diving in the salt-water pool at the Victoria Recreation Club, VRC.

My mother and her Chinese tennis partner, Mary Chow, who was also her close friend, were unbeatable doubles champions against every Hong Kong club. Both were fighters who practiced long hours and never gave up! KCC, unlike the racist inclination of The Shanghai Club, was accepting of all races.

Through sheer luck, I too won the doubles championship when I drew one of the strongest KGV tennis partners, Gillian, who played almost every winning shot, and—without much help from me—secured the match, scoring 6-2, 6-2, 7-5. I knew she was unhappy to have drawn my name, but felt a lot better after we left the court as winners!

My parents met and befriended some of the military and naval personnel stationed in Hong Kong—homesick young men who enjoyed spending time with a family. They were made very welcome in our home. Once, when I was twelve, two sailors who were frequently our guests— one very short, and the other about six feet tall—came over when only us kids were home. Somehow, on some pretext, they got me into my parents' bedroom. The bigger one grabbed, and tried to kiss and fondle me. Terrified, I fought him off like a tiger, managing somehow to snatch my mother's red lipstick from her dressing table and smearing it all over him. He was furious! They left in a hurry.

My fourteen-year-old brother and younger sister, in the living room, were completely unaware of my ordeal! Where, oh where, was Ah Loy, our Amah?

I had been in imminently real danger and was thoroughly frightened! After that episode I realized instinctively that something had changed. I was starting to develop, and about to acquire my first bra. I became extra-vigilant—things would obviously never be the same again.

From then on, whenever so-called sailor "friends" rang our doorbell we refused them entry, saying from behind the closed door, "Our parents are out—we can't let you in." Soon they stopped "dropping in" uninvited. My parents, hitherto really rather naïve and over-trusting, made sure the opportunity never arose again for such abuse of their hospitality.

In a nearby adjacent building, separated from us by a narrow alley, I could see directly into several floors of apartments. On each level something different was taking place. I listened to incessant loud chattering of Chinese tenants and their friends, many of them wizened, with straggly, sparse white beards. Some ancient-looking women swayed in and out of rooms on painfully bound feet.

I watched people playing cards and mahjong in dimly lit rooms. Their tiles clicked loudly throughout the night, and money changed hands many times. They chewed seeds, constantly spitting out husks. They hawked and spat into colorful ceramic spittoons. Steaming, aromatic Chinese food was delivered periodically from the kitchen, where, through an adjacent window, I had seen servants preparing it. How I wished I could have some of the delicious-smelling offerings!

In one apartment, dazed opium smokers lay languidly on low

wooden beds, the floor, or draped over anything that could hold them, while they obliterated the world. Fascinated, I wondered whether any of them were aware of my obvious interest in their activities, or even of my regular presence.

From time to time I seemed to detect some amused glances in my direction—from those I observed for such long hours. Perhaps, because I was just a young girl, I posed no threat.

A little way up the hill, on our street, Chinese, many of them menial laborers and Rickshaw pullers, could go into squalid dens in narrow alleys and pay very little to smoke a pipe. The opium was cooked over a small alcohol burner. A blob of it, collected on a slowly twirled metal wire, was then twirled again rapidly over a flame. Smoke emanated from the blob, and this was passed over the bowl of the pipe a few times. The addict breathed in deeply until his eyes glazed over, and he fell into a deep hypnotic sleep.

I walked past darkened dens sometimes, and could faintly discern sprawling bodies, languishing in total, blissful oblivion. The air in surrounding alleyways was thick with the smoke and acrid smell of the debilitating narcotic.

In the late nineteenth century, two out of three Hong Kong Chinese had smoked opium. The government sold an annual opium monopoly until the drug was finally outlawed in 1940.

# SECRET SOCIETY ASPIRATIONS

An audition date was announced for the annual school play. I was excited—it was almost certain I would be selected. One way or another, I was always involved in dance, theatre, and music, and generally acknowledged as artistically talented. I was stunned when I didn't get any part in the production.

Heartbroken, I attended every single rehearsal, sitting in the front row of the empty hall. I couldn't understand why I wasn't chosen. I felt acutely rejected. Still, I sat there alone, memorizing every word of the play—longing to be part of it.

On the day of the performance, the leading actress suddenly became extremely ill and was hospitalized! The producer was frantic. "What are we going to do?" she wailed.

"I'll do it," I announced. "I can do it—I know every word of the play." And indeed, I was the only possible replacement. So—magically—I became the star of the show!

We had Scottish dancing lessons with Miss McNeil, a newer teacher at our school. Soon it was obvious she and Mr. Mulcahy, our vice principal, had more than a passing professional interest in each other. They were both seemingly reserved people, and blushed easily. We watched, giggling and speculating, as their romance unfolded and finally culminated in their engagement and marriage. For school kids it was an exciting event.

Mr. Mulcahy was one of my favorite teachers, and seemed to know about my peer difficulties. He always treated me very kindly, praising my achievements, and strengthening my self-esteem. In complete contrast, the history and geography teachers gave me a really difficult time, picking on me incessantly, no matter how I fared in those subjects. Discouraged, I made hardly any effort to improve my marks. "Ester Benjamin," the geography teacher, hair tightly coifed and lips pursed, never failed to scold, loudly, "*HOW* many times must I describe the Mediterranean climate to you?"

Ironically, I eventually spent most of my teen years basking in that very wonderfully sunny climate! I suspect she returned to England to spend the rest of her days in some city that should, during incessantly inclement weather, have had a roof over it!

I was still an avid reader of Enid Blyton's *Famous Five,* and *Secret Seven* series. She was my favorite author, and I fantasized being one of her heroes—or one of the girls at boarding school, enjoying forbidden midnight parties!

I also loved *Nancy Drew* and *The Hardy Boys* series, created by American author, Edward Stratemeyer. We were fortunate to be exposed to a diversified group of international writers.

Mr. Ferguson, our stern headmaster, was soon to be transferred to the Education Office, and would be replaced by Mr. Mulcahy—which made me very happy. Before Mr. Ferguson left the school I asked for an audience, and approached him rather fearlessly with a grand idea that had been mulling around in my head since being planted there by one of Enid Blyton's book series.

"Mr. Ferguson," I said, losing some of my nerve, "I want to ask permission for a few of us to use the Pavilion as a meeting place."

"What kind of meeting place?" he asked, looking both a little surprised and interested at the same time.

"To start a secret society—like the one in Enid Blyton's books."

I think he was amused. He appeared to lose his usually stern demeanor. The side of his mouth twitched, raising his understated handlebar moustache slightly as he fought a smile. "Oh, I don't think that would be possible," he said kindly. Seeing my disappointment, he added quickly, "If I allow *you* to use the Pavilion, I won't be able to refuse anyone else who asks me. I'm sure you understand why I have to say 'no,' my dear."

And that terminated my secret society aspirations!

We also read a lot of American comics—bought at the Chinese news vendor's stall, and exchanged for others when finished. Dagwood and Blondie Bumstead, Archie, Captain Marvel, and Little Lulu, were amongst our favorite choices. Mummy loved comics as much as we did. She was a prolific, eclectic reader, and always said, "Everything you read can teach you something—even comics." And I think she was right. She derived so much enjoyment from reading them, while lying on her bed during the day, and intermittently laughing out loudly, as we all did, easily seeing humor in many situations. She read up to four books a week and always had a formidable word-power!

My father only read non-fiction, and never held a comic in his hands, unless he was tidying up! Although he was prone to mood swings, he *did* have a great sense of humor—it just wasn't always that obvious.

We had a mongrel dog, Bonnie, that once had a litter. I don't remember what happened to her puppies, but I *do* remember acquiring a motherless kitten that Bonnie claimed as her new baby. It was a real sight to see her actually suckling and nurturing a kitten!

We were not allowed to feed the dog at the table, and Daddy, who was not a true pet-lover, threatened to get rid of her if she persisted in begging for food during our mealtimes. When she continued to hover around, David solved the problem by feeding her some chili sauce! She ran away howling and never returned to the dinner table. One day Bonnie disappeared. Surprisingly, Daddy, apparently really upset by our loss, helped us search nearby roads and accompanied us to the police station in hopes of finding our dog. We had no luck. In China it was hard to know the real fate of a missing pet.

Our Amah, Ah Loy, had a little room near the kitchen, at the back of our apartment. A woman friend often visited, and slept with her. Everything about their relationship raised our suspicions that they were lesbians—not an uncommon situation. I spent quite a lot of time in Ah Loy's room, listening to them chattering and giggling. Once, she was preparing a stretchy pastry for one of Mummy's fried specialties. She rolled it until it was really long, and then, shrieking with laughter, held it against her pubic area and swung it round and round. Her girlfriend, overcome with mirth, fell to the floor! They said something I didn't understand, and collapsed again with loud, hysterical peals of laughter!

## NATHAN ROAD

Nathan Road, a well-known main artery in Kowloon, was very close to our apartment and only a few blocks from the Star Ferry Terminal. I loved all the interesting bargain shops I passed, that carried everything—from fabrics, cameras, pearls and jade, to inlaid furniture, intricately carved ivory, and more. Ignoring the din, I watched coolies carrying bamboo shoulder poles and hawkers peddling wares, as I walked down to the celebrated Peninsula Hotel that commanded an unrivaled, sweeping view of the harbor and Victoria Peak. It was close to shops where, for a low price, one could order custom-made suits and shoes, completed and delivered within twenty-four hours. Many dignitaries, Hollywood stars, and famous people stayed there when visiting the colony.

Once, hearing actor Tyrone Power was staying at the Peninsula for a few days, I ran down to the hotel and stood at his door, without hindrance, for about three hours, patiently awaiting his return. He was surprised to see me, and graciously signed his autograph on the sheet of paper I supplied. It was very exciting!

"I'm going to live in Hollywood one day," I announced, with conviction. "Sure you are," he said, patting me on the head patronizingly, "sure you are," he repeated, "why not?" I have no idea what he was *really* thinking!

Little did either of us know that, after harboring this ambition since early childhood, I would indeed eventually live near Hollywood, in Los

Angeles! I had envisioned myself living in the United States and had modeled myself on swimming star Esther Williams, gathering friends to swim around me in elaborate "Hollywood style" formations. I was honored when they called me by her name when I won races. Sixty years later I had an opportunity to meet and speak with the aging star, who, on that occasion, was seated in a wheel chair. My childhood fantasy fell flat when my story did not seem to impress her as much as I had hoped. But, by this time I was no longer awe-struck by stardom, and rather bored with the self-importance of the famous.

My father's three cousins and their mother also stayed at the Peninsula Hotel when they passed through Hong Kong on their way to Canada and the USA. I went to say a last goodbye to them. Somehow—despite internment in Shanghai—they had maintained their affluence.

My first beloved peeing-doll had been a cast-off gift from cousin Mona, for which I was grateful beyond measure. My brother had spent many childhood hours playing with cousin Albert's cast-off toy lead soldiers. David was constantly scolded by Mummy for sucking on them. I suspect lead poisoning might have contributed in some measure to his learning difficulties at the time.

Sadly, although we all live in North America, my attempts at reuniting with my cousins were inexplicably unsuccessful.

I often admired the ingenuity of people who managed to hold onto their wealth throughout the war years, and the innovative ways and means they used to clandestinely shift money and jewels out of Communist-run Shanghai. Thrilling stories were emerging out of the woodwork—one of them from my Uncle Syddie, who was on board the ship carrying him to Hong Kong when he was alerted that all cabins were being searched for "contraband" money. He sat on his bed reading a newspaper when the authorities burst into his room. "What money do you have?" they demanded to know.

"Nothing," he answered. "You told us we were not allowed to have any money."

"Well," they said, "we're going to search anyway."

"Ok," my uncle said. He threw the folded newspaper on the bed and left the cabin.

After they left he returned, picked up the newspaper, opened it, and found all his concealed money still snuggly intact!

In another instance, our friends, a large family traveling by train, told us their story: They were allowed to leave with only the barest necessities and sufficient food for the journey, so they prepared a large saucepan of curry, and ate some of it every time the guards came by. Upon arrival at their final destination, they removed the curried remnants from the large pot, carefully unwrapped the brown wax paper drumsticks and thighs, and exposed the riches they had so ingeniously concealed! Their clever thinking enabled them to buy a beautiful apartment in Israel.

David and I were usually the only children catching the public double-decker bus to school. Sometimes an elderly Ceylonese woman in a long dark grey coat, her silver hair severely pulled back in a bun, stood at the corner, close to the Nathan and Granville Road bus stop. She always approached me when I was alone, questioning, "Where do you live pretty girl? What's your name? Would you like to go somewhere very nice with me?"

"No," I answered—frightened, and sensing something evil about the woman. She always seemed to await my sole arrival. "I'm waiting for my father. He's arriving any moment now. I think I see him." Sometimes I told her my father worked in the police department. To my great relief her appearances dwindled until she eventually disappeared altogether.

Nothing deterred me from roaming freely and catching public transport and ferries on my own. I had learnt to be extremely alert and aware of my surroundings.

Hong Kong Chinese differed in subtle ways from those of Shanghai. Inscrutable, and hardly smiling, they appeared unfriendly and even hostile towards foreigners. With good reason, they resented the British colonization. Added to that, they had suffered several years of occupation after the Japanese overran Hong Kong in just two weeks in 1941.

Few foreigners took the trouble to learn Cantonese, a singsong language with—depending on the intonation—different meanings to the same word. Being able to converse with our Chinese friends and neighbors was both extremely enjoyable and favorable. Mummy, not particularly fluent in the language, was easily able to have a Chinese tennis partner because we were partial to, and accepting of, our host country's people. They trusted us.

I had the pleasure of being invited to tell my class about Chinese customs and culture. Their ignorance amazed me! They were fascinated, and asked a lot of questions. I felt fortunate my father had shared so much information about China and its people. As well, living amongst the

Chinese helped me understand their culture and enjoy their food. Many foreigners lived a fairly isolated life on Victoria Peak, and only traveled down for work or shopping excursions. In Hong Kong, the higher you lived on the Peak, the higher your status in society was deemed to be.

My parents befriended people very easily and loved to entertain, inviting friends and business acquaintances over for cocktails—a favorite pastime in colonial oriented China. Martinis, gin and tonic, vermouth, whisky, brandy and other drinks flowed freely. No one would ever guess how Mummy, on a low budget, prepared all the delicious special foods— vegetable cutlets, curry and rice, fried pastries, and other "dainties." Guests gobbled everything up at high speed! Her culinary skills were legendary.

# ADOLESCENCE

All my school uniforms were made to order by Chinese tailors. Mummy bought the fabrics from shops in alleys, where prices were so much less than elsewhere. I loved my white, short-sleeved summer uniform. I felt cool wearing it during the long hot summer. Our brown blazer's pocket badge was embroidered with the lion and motto, *Honestas Ante Honores*. We couldn't afford to buy it from the school supply store, so Mummy matched the brown woolen fabric very carefully with the official blazer. The selected color was a lovely, warmer shade of brown. It was perfectly tailored, and no one ever commented on the slight difference in hue. Perhaps other postwar, economically challenged children were in a similar situation.

Compared with the sylph-like English girls, I was rather chubby. We ate a lot of fried and starchy food. Most days when I returned from school I ate rice and soy sauce. I loved it, but had no idea how much it contributed to my rounded frame. I also seemed to be developing at a faster rate than my classmates and felt extremely self-conscious. On the rare occasions when invited to a party, although I always wore a beautifully homemade dress, it did nothing to improve my self-image. I would shrink into the background, nursing my thoughts and anxieties. I have a painful memory of one occasion in particular. I wore a beautiful, darkish royal blue, shiny taffeta two-piece dress with shoulder straps, in the "new look," mid-calf length of the day. I felt chunky, clunky, and miserable, and was ignored by everyone! That day, I realized sadly that the pretentious, snobby, wealthy, racist colonials, with their assumed air of superiority, would never accept me. I just didn't fit in. I would have to look after myself and develop inner resources.

During this time, my father was dealing with the sudden decision of his mother and brother to emigrate to England. He was struggling to keep the business going, and was surprised and stunned by the news of their imminent departure. He felt they were leaving him in the lurch—"holding the baby," so to speak. The grief of that parting accompanied my father his whole life. "My mother just walked away from me," he said, dejectedly.

None of us ever saw them again. It hurt a lot over the years…

From England, my grandmother and uncle relocated to Sydney, Australia, where they, and all my father's sisters, eventually spent the rest of their lives.

One day Mummy decided we would all go for a walk on Kadoorie Avenue, an exclusive residential area built on a hill. We walked up and down the roads, admiring the lovely homes. We stopped suddenly on Braga Circuit, in front of a totally neglected semi-detached, double-storey house, in dire need of a new coat of paint! It was obviously unoccupied. The windows were shuttered, and the garden overgrown.

"This is it!" Mummy exclaimed excitedly. "This is the house I saw in my dream!"

My mother wasted no time contacting the Kadoorie property management office. "Although I never asked for it, we got the house at a considerably lowered rent," she said. "I'm sure it's because Kadoorie knew our family well. He was a patron and benefactor of the Girl Guides, and knew I was leader of the Ninth Company in Shanghai."

Overjoyed, we moved into Braga Circuit, and happily set to work restoring the house to good order. We bought a large Westinghouse fridge, a washing machine and other appliances. Mummy's friends, Prissy, Mary Chow, and others, came over to share the pleasure of our new surroundings. We sat in the garden, and in true colonial style, enjoyed mid-morning elevenses and late-afternoon high tea, offering cucumber sandwiches, cake and cool drinks. Daddy invited people for cocktails. It seemed things were finally looking up.

A wealthy Chinese family with a tennis court lived around the corner from us. Mummy befriended them and was occasionally invited to participate in their games. We went with her and watched them play.

I don't know how she fared so well against them. Their inscrutable facial expressions never changed! It was impossible to see where they intended to place the ball—they never looked in the direction where the confounding ball landed!

Everyone ate Chinese pastries and drank iced tea from a huge silver container that was constantly refilled by servants, who seemed to know exactly when to emerge from the house with replenishments.

My father never drank cold tea—he was obsessed with the correct preparation of *hot* tea. "You must pour boiling water on the leaves," he said, demonstrating every step many times over the years. He always covered the dragon-embossed, silver teapot with a tea cozy. "It has to stand for a few minutes before pouring," he instructed, before serving the delicious, perfect brew. The teapot was a wedding present, lovingly kept and constantly used since 1935. It took him many years to agree to use teabags. "I'm a man of habit," he would announce proudly, wearing his limitation like a badge of honor!

Although Braga Circuit was an elegant, desirable address, Kadoorie Avenue was, for me, very isolated. There was only one accessible roadway, and every day we walked down several steps to catch the school bus on the main road. I missed the excitement and bustle of Granville Road with its close proximity to shops and ferries.

# YIP THE GYP

Daddy came home earlier than usual from the office. His face was blanched. "Yip has gone!" he said.

"What do you mean—gone?" Mummy asked.

"He took everything—sold it all," he said, plopping down into the nearest armchair.

Mummy looked shocked. "I don't understand! What happened?"

"We just had no business, and I don't know what happened... Yip was a crook! He sold someone's cargo in the warehouse, paid everybody's salaries with the proceeds, and bunked it."

"How did he get away with it?" I asked.

"We had so many bags, and bags, and bags, of flour—he gave the delivery order to take it out, sold it, took the money, and paid all the workers. The police came looking for him. 'Where's Yip?' they asked me. I said, 'I really can't tell you.'"

"Yip knew this was the end of us. He used to be good..." My father was overcome by the shock of the betrayal, and how this would affect our lives. His hopes for recovery in the business world were dashed.

*He absconded with everything*! I thought, trying to work out what this really meant. I remembered Mr. Yip filling the wicker suitcase with our personal valuables and silver items. Much of what we entrusted him with, for safekeeping during our internment, was missing when we were freed. He said it had been stolen.

Previously, when I asked my father about our valuables he said, quite forgivingly, "Yip may have sold it to buy food—many people had no money during the war." He had no idea his trusted Comprador was a wily crook that would one day stab him in the back!

A very difficult time followed. We lived in a lovely home, but were once again exceedingly short of money and struggling to survive.

To compound matters, in June 1950 North Korea invaded South Korea, with disastrous effect for business in Hong Kong. An international United Nations military coalition, headed by the United States, dispatched forces to assist the beleaguered South.

Many years after we left Hong Kong, I sat with my parents and recorded the following account of how the embargo affected us.

"What actually happened that caused you to lose your livelihood in Hong Kong?" I asked my father.

"The United Nations declared war on Korea. General Mc Arthur led the war," he said. "When it intensified, the United States and Allies started placing embargoes on Hong Kong. They didn't want cargo coming in."

"Why not? What was the problem?" Until now I had only heard vague references to the Korean War. I was too young and naïve at the time to understand the ramifications of the conflict and subsequent embargo.

"For example, the Chinese would come at night, saying they were just bringing junks—carrying cargo up and down. But they would buy eight or ten tires, and tie them alongside, as though these were only bumpers against the wharves. But the tires would really be used for tanks. What came to Hong Kong went through the back door to Macau, and to the Communists."

My father couldn't pay the exorbitant rentals. He told the warehouse owner to just take all my grandmother's furniture and goods that had been shipped from Shanghai, to defray costs.

"So—all that stuff that was left in the warehouse—was it your godown, and you just left it there—that's it?" I asked my father.

"The furniture was there. You don't know how much we owed the landlord—two, three months rent—and I couldn't pay. We had to pay $2000 a month for a warehouse of 21,000 square feet, 7000 square feet on each floor. No cargo in, and no cargo out. Embargo! And $2000 a month—I don't know how I got out of it..." He still sounded desperate while relating the details.

"And the other one, Benjy? You had two places—did you forget?" my mother reminded him.

"Yes—the other one was smaller. I said to myself, 'The Hell with everybody, I'm going to get out on my own, and nobody is going to have anything on me. Finished! Let them take the damn thing and burn it up!'"

"All the lovely blackwood furniture which your brother put in storage in Shanghai—where was it?" My mother asked, apparently having forgotten the details.

"In the big warehouse in Hong Kong. Everything in huge cases— and all left there…"

"She got it all out of Shanghai? Blackwood—all gone? God almighty!" Mummy exclaimed.

"Liza," my father said, "better that happened—than my life would be gone."

This was a revelation. I had no idea the furniture I saw in the Shanghai warehouse had been shipped out. Now I wondered aloud, "Could they have got it out of Hong Kong as well?"

"They had no more interest," he said. "They went to England for a couple of years. Syddie made quite a lot of money as a travelling salesman— electrical-parts guy. He went from town to town, buying and selling small items. Then they visited Australia and liked the place, so they moved there." My father's sister, Eva, went with them.

"Did they ever try to find out what happened to us after they left?" I asked.

"Never! They're dead to me," he said bitterly. Most of the time my father seemed to manage, somehow, to effectively obliterate painful memories. I wondered, *was that really possible? What was the actual lifelong toll exacted?* Our poor family had been shredded apart.

"So, was I going to die because of *furniture?* I told the Landlord 'I'm getting out—I have nothing more to pay. Such high rent—you took enough!' He killed us with the damn rent."

"So," I reflected, "He took it all—and probably would have taken it anyway. Could that have been a good business if everything had gone well?"

"Hong Kong was a bloody dead man's land—rubbish! Garbage! I got no salary and had a lot to worry about." Decades later, the memory still evoked resentment. Was recalling what happened cathartic for my father? He often brooded over his difficult life.

"You know how much it must be valued at now?" he asked.

"But it was not my luck," he added. "My luck was to get out alive!"

# LAST DAYS IN CHINA

In August 1950, my mother's parents and most of her immediate family decided to emigrate to the newly declared State of Israel. My mother was overcome by the difficult parting. Her brother Isaac's family had departed earlier, on the *Wooster Victory*, the same ship that carried two of my father's sisters' families to the nascent State.

"So many separations," I said to my father.

"Yes—we all said goodbye many times…" he answered sadly. "Not only us. Many people were emigrating to foreign countries."

Since Mao Zedong had taken over the mainland in 1949, the massive influx of Nationalists and supporters fleeing China had greatly strained Hong Kong's already struggling resources.

In 1951, motivated by the U.S. embargo, Hong Kong's economy shifted enterprisingly, from distribution and storage to manufacturing.

My father made a valiant effort to recover from his business setbacks, but found it too challenging to start over again. He encountered many obstacles in the rapidly changing face of the China he knew and loved.

"I can't do it Liza," he said, holding his head in his hands in despair.

"What do you think we should do?" She, too, appeared to have no answers.

"I don't think we will ever make it again in China. This war will not end now—we have no way of recovering from our losses."

"Then, if that's true, why don't we go to Israel?" My mother's question was really a life-changing statement that stunned us all! We knew she missed her family terribly, but had no idea this thought may have been germinating since their departure in 1950.

"Liza—how can we do that? Don't talk nonsense! I have too many things to do here before we could leave. It's a mess."

The idea of leaving our new home before we had even lived in it four months was inconceivable to us children. *How could that happen*? I wondered. At the same time, there was an exciting element in the thought of joining our relatives, and helping to develop our new Jewish homeland. Israel was assisting newcomers and encouraging immigration in every possible way. It was the perfect choice—not that we really had one, being financially incapable of funding a move to any other country.

My mother was an ardent Zionist, and my religiously observant father never missed an opportunity to spout biblical wisdom. He often controlled us by invoking threats of divine retribution for our misdemeanors! He would fit right in, with his strict ideas about upbringing and misbehavior.

"We'll leave first," my mother said, taking control of the matter. She was the Guide Leader, and we were her patrol! "You can finish off here without hindrance and join us later, as soon as you can get away." She made it sound easy! Her mind was firmly made up, and she brooked none of my father's objections.

Once the decision was made, my mother wasted no time contacting the Jewish Agency. The paperwork and fine details were taken care of with whirlwind speed. Once again the house was alive with activity. We sold, or gave away, furniture and everything else that would be of no future use to us. Mummy packed trunks full of essentials to be shipped. We went shopping to Wing On's and other large department stores. It was July—seasonal sales and bargains abounded. My mother cleverly purchased clothing and shoes in sizes we could grow into. She bought a Brother sewing machine and lengths of fabric for later creative use. She thought everything out with clarity, carried out all her ideas and plans speedily and precisely, and accomplished everything in under two weeks!

The new Westinghouse fridge, washing machine, and other electrical appliances, all of which were in short supply, and extremely expensive to purchase in Israel, would be shipped. Our Monington and Weston piano was carefully crated for the long voyage. I had only recently, at age thirteen, started my first "official" piano lessons with Pearl, a lovely Ceylonese teacher. I had played everything hitherto by ear, imitating, and learning whatever I could from cousins and musical friends.

My earliest jazz lessons were from watching and copying basic boogie-woogie techniques, at the YMCA and elsewhere, played by musical GIs who liberated us from camp. I had somehow received from them two small, fat songbooks containing lyrics of hundreds of popular songs. I played the piano and sang at every opportunity.

The realization suddenly hit me with enormous force. *We're really going to leave—without my father!*

Many last minute details had to be attended to. Neither David nor I had matriculated yet. Our principal couldn't understand why we would leave before the end of the 1951 academic year. Our future schooling prospects seemed uncertain.

It was an enormous leap of faith. My mother was really very brave, even though she had her family to welcome her at the end of the journey. As for my father—I can only guess at the turmoil he endured. He would have no support system after we left, and had to face alone, and solve, many problems before he could join us. Seeing his despair, I feared for his well-being.

I was also aware of trying to commit to memory everything peculiar to China—the people, food, smells, and sounds—that could never, nor would it ever, be convincingly duplicated elsewhere.

Many friends, saddened by our pending departure, came over to say goodbye, shed tears, and exchange promises—that mostly never materialized—to stay in touch. Happily, Mary Chow decided she loved our house enough to pay key money and take it over from us. Sadly, she lost touch with Mummy after we left Hong Kong.

With the speed of lightning, the day of departure loomed largely over us. It became increasingly harder to face the reality of the last difficult hours before parting from my father. He would be lodging at the YMCA until his own departure, four months later—if all went as planned.


We took a taxi to Kai Tak Airport, in Kowloon, named after two businessmen, Sir Ho Kai and Mr. Au Tak. In 1942 the occupying Japanese army had expanded the airport, using Allied prisoners of war. They labored long grueling hours, building two concrete runways. In the process, they destroyed the historic wall of the Kowloon Walled City.

Rugged mountains surrounded the area. Pilots had to exercise great skill in making a sharp left turn soon after take-off, to avoid the hills and the island's second highest peak—Mount Parker—right in front of the aircraft. Notwithstanding the airport's challenging topography, relatively few accidents occurred.

By the strangest coincidence, after a long, tedious journey, we would arrive in Israel on August 7, exactly one year to the day after my mother's family landed there in 1950.

Two young girls walked into the departure lounge and looked around. I couldn't believe my eyes—they were the very same classmates who had so relentlessly bullied me at school! *What were they doing here? They couldn't possibly be travelling somewhere today*, I thought. *Probably came to see someone off.*

They walked straight up to me. "Hello Ester," they greeted me warmly. "We've come to say goodbye, and to wish you *bon voyage* and good luck in Israel."

I was completely overcome by waves of conflicting emotions. These girls had caused me endless hours of pain and anguish! "Thank you very much," I said, hesitantly, "it's nice of you to come to the airport." I didn't know what to say *or* think.

"We're really very sorry for being so mean to you. We'll miss you," Susan said. The other girl nodded in agreement. Ironically, her uncle had been employed in my father's business in Hong Kong. Some relatives of both girls had also already departed for other countries. So many people were saying "goodbye" to friends and family.

Until now I had managed to be quite strong about leaving, telling myself I would never miss KGV, and all the miserable times I endured at the hands of my classmates. I felt tears stinging my eyes. It was all too much! I could see the girls were also fighting tears. Then they asked questions about my impending journey and new life in Israel, and once again, for the last time, we were just three young, excited, "chatty" schoolgirls.

It was time to board. I don't quite remember details of how we got through those last frantic, emotional moments before embarking. Many kisses, hugs, tears, promises, bags, and shouts later, we mounted the steps and were seated.

I looked out the window and saw Daddy standing forlornly with many others bidding farewell. We waved to each other.

The engines were revving up, and too soon, we cleared the runway and were airborne. The airplane made the essential sixty-five degree sharp turn to safety, and everyone breathed a sigh of relief. The sparkling ocean came clearly into view. Wharves, ships, sampans, and junks diminished in size until they were dots. The mountain ranges faded into the distance. It was clear flying ahead.

I felt my heart lurch with excitement. Three years ago I had said *Zai hui*, goodbye, to Shanghai.

Now, as the craft drew farther and farther away, I said wistfuly, this time in Cantonese, *Joigin Hoeng Gong—baaibaai.*

Goodbye Hong Kong, *Fragrant Harbor.* Farewell China—forever.

2005 BBC One, We'll Meet Again. Ex-child internees with Belfast sailors.

Front row, L to R: Militza Srivastava, Anne Moxley, Ester Shifren, three sailors: John Whithouse, Bill Shaw, Victor Padri.

Back Row L to R: Ron Blyth, Rodney Stableford, Joan Bulley, Jose Chamberlain, Ian Pearson, Carol Channing, Barrie Martin, Richard Germain.

L to R. Ester, Anna Fowler and BBC ONE team. Reunion party 2005.

# LONDON 2005: WE'LL MEET AGAIN

"Did you realize how much it had meant to those 'children?'"

Des Lynam's question to the three *HMS Belfast* sailors jolts me back to the moment. I'm sitting tensely on the edge of my seat. A quick glance shows me all ten "children" are leaning forward, eyes riveted on the brightly lit stage.

Some hours earlier we had all been chauffeured in style to the BBC studio, where, sixty years after the war, we were reunited with fellow internees, and met some "children" for the first time. Although interned in various camps, we had all experienced an immediate feeling of camaraderie, and hugged each other warmly. I recognized names, but not the faces of the ones from my own camps—they had shared such a potent, meaningful segment of my early childhood. We verbally charged down long forgotten passages of time, noisily sharing camp memories of mutual friends, games we played, schooling, and our deprivation and hunger. We exchanged contact details, and cameras flashed as we endeavored to close the gap of lost years. The air in our cozy meeting-room had positively bristled with energy!

Carefully orchestrating fine details leading to our studio entry, Anna Fowler had thrilled and honored me when she said, "Ester—you will have the special privilege of sitting next to the sailors and thanking them. You're not time restricted. Just use descriptive words and speak from your heart." I was so thankful I had decided to wear my beautiful gold and multi-colored

Asian Jacket as a special finishing touch. I was ready!

On cue, with a heightened feeling of excitement and anticipation, we filed down the steps into the studio, accompanied by the increasing swell of the show's signature tune, *We'll Meet Again*. Many in the audience were singing along and clapping.

Des Lynam's question—*Did you realize how much it had meant to those "children?"*—has given the men pause. They look thoughtful for a moment.

"No, I don't think we did," replies one of the three. He was the ship's cook in 1945. "It meant a lot to us, mind. It's so nice to know they still remember it, sixty years later," Looking dignified and slightly solemn, the men—John, Bill, and Victor—are adorned with war decorations and ribbons, and appropriately attired for the program commemorating the 60th anniversary of Victory in Europe day.

Des asks, "What special memory do you have, Bill?"

"The children coming on board," Bill says, smiling. "After all they'd been deprived of in their young lives, to suddenly be invited on board a ship to a party—to have some fun. But I believe, in the first instance they were shocked, but once they got on board all inhibitions went, and all of us joined in the fun and thoroughly enjoyed ourselves. Every one of us, I'm sure."

Des addresses the audience, "Now—victory in Europe meant that hundreds of thousands of troops could return home and try to restart their lives, but with Japan still fighting, the war continued to rage in the Far East. One group greatly affected by this was the allied families who had been living and working in China at the time it fell under Japanese occupation. A large number of these families were in Shanghai, and more than half of those taken prisoner were children."

*We were those child prisoners—he's talking about us!* I think to myself. I exchange glances with the other "children." I suspect we're attempting to gauge one another's reactions—straining to identify the painfully undernourished children in the riveting on-screen photographs and movie clips of internees. Scenes of *HMS Belfast* sailing into Shanghai's busy harbor, accompanied by sampans and tugboats, and personnel visiting the camps in 1945, alternate with our own recent BBC interviews.

Waves of sadness overcome me as I recall Yu Yuen Road camp, the ex-Shanghai public school of my mother's own childhood days. With sudden new insight, I wonder to myself—*did she find the familiar surroundings comforting? Could that partially explain her positive attitude and unique optimism during such punishing times?*

Des continues, "The captain and crew spent the first few days visiting former internees ashore. Many families were still living in the camps—as they had nowhere else to go. The crew was shocked by the conditions they found, but impressed by the resolve the prisoners had shown while detained. The *Belfast* sailors, desperate to do something for the children, decided to throw a party on board the ship."

Turning, he asks, "What prompted you to throw the party?"

"These kids hadn't had a childhood," Bill says, sadly. "They'd been pushed around from pillar to post and had a really horrible time. All they knew was the deprivation they'd had—what they'd been through in their young lives. We wanted to give them something back."

"So," Des says, "at the end of September 1945, for the first time in three years, the young Shanghai internees were able to celebrate."

The ex-cook says, smiling, "We were faced with an overwhelming request for jelly and managed to prepare some in a great hurry!"

Laughing, Des says, "Well, eleven of the children—now a few years older—are here to say a personal 'thank you' for that day sixty years ago. You've always stayed in their memories and hearts, and we're about to reunite them with you. They're here in our audience." Waving in our direction he says, "Please come down and join us."

The band strikes up the signature tune. Walking slowly, accompanied by thunderous applause, we reach the stage and shake hands with the three completely surprised, misty-eyed ex-sailors. Obviously emotionally challenged by our unexpected appearance, their eyes glisten as they struggle to keep their composure—very evidently applying to the best of their ability, a "stiff British upper lip." Many visibly moved spectators are blowing noses and wiping tears.

As Anna had promised, I'm sitting right next to the sailors, in the front of two small rows.

Des says, "One of the children we saw in the film is Ester Shifren. She's flown in from Los Angeles to be here tonight, and on behalf of all the children who were at the *Belfast* party, I know that, Ester, you'd like to say a few words, wouldn't you?"

*I'm unprepared*, I think to myself, *what am I going to say?* My heart is pounding with excitement. I turn to the three elderly gentlemen, and, without hesitation, the words just tumble out of my mouth! "I would like to say, on behalf of all of us here, how absolutely wonderful it was of you to have us on the ship. I remember going up the gangplank and seeing all of you in white uniforms, looking so wonderful—and how the sailors got down on their knees so they were the same height as us, to greet and welcome us on board. The loving feeling they gave us—that we were loved and secure, and the war was *really* over, and it's just—I never thought the day would come that we could thank you. Thank you so very, very much."

Ester at HMS Belfast reunion party in 2005.

Reception at Westminster 2005: Ester with General Sir Michael Walker, at the time Chief of Defence Staff, UK Armed Forces.

# DÉJÀ VU PARTY ON THE *HMS BELFAST*

In August 2005, after a long flight from Los Angeles, I've returned to London to attend the re-creation of the 1945 "children's" party on the *HMS Belfast*. The event is one of several commemorating the 60th anniversary of VJ (Victory Japan) day. The Befast, now permanently docked on the Thames, is part of the Imperial War Museum. As their guest, for the next ten days I'll be giving daily talks on board and at the main museum.

I feel surprisingly refreshed after having a good night's sleep and hearty breakfast. Umbrella in hand, I leave the Tower Bridge Hotel, walk past the Tower of London, across the imposing bridge, and down the South Bank to a warm welcome on board by Brad King, the *Belfast* Director. The atmosphere is festive; the ship has been decorated with a skirt of flags representing every country, with the exception of Japan, in readiness for the next afternoon's party.

I am overcome with emotion and excitement and feel a rush of nostalgia when I see replications of the 1945 party—a swing, bosun's chair, and huge box-swing that we "children" of '45 had enjoyed so much after our horrific internment.

My anticipated first BBC interview is unexpectedly rescheduled for the following morning, so after a while I leave the ship and make my way back, walking past crowded bars and restaurants at Saint Catherine's Dock. The weather is glorious, and many people are milling about on the banks and bridges.

Feeling a little hungry, I walk into a food store, looking randomly for something to eat. I find myself standing next to a family, parents and two teenagers, in front of a bewildering array of delicious-looking bread. They are carrying some bulging paper bags and bottles of wine.

"Hello," I say, striking up a conversation, "Which one of these loaves do you recommend?"

"We're just visiting London on our private boat, so we're also new to this selection," the mother says, in a friendly tone. "Where are you from, and what are you doing in London?"

"I'm from Los Angeles," I say, and tell them about the *Belfast* party.

"We've heard about that—it's been on the news," the father says, adding, "why don't you join us for a snack on our boat? We'll be back there in about half an hour's time." He gives me directions.

I'm really happy for the opportunity— there are still some hours of daylight left, and I feel rather lonely wandering around on my own. I eventually wend my way to them, and we spend a delightful time on deck, talking and sipping wine while the sun sinks slowly out of sight.

On Saturday, defying a rainy forecast, the weather is crisp, cool and dry. From Tower Bridge, the majestic, flag-encircled ship looks resplendent.

HMS Belfast decorated in 2005 for re-enacted 1945 tea party.

Cameramen and reporters begin arriving on board at 8:30 a.m. Throughout the day I am interviewed about the internment, and

Ester Back on the HMS Belfast swing in 2005.

photographed on, or beside, the swing that is hooked up. The picture of me swinging at the original party is fixed to the nearby wall. I feel euphoric, and can hardly believe the luck that brought me to this wonderful reunion.

Excitement peaks and voices rise to a clamor, as over one hundred "children" of the 1945 party, and guests, arrive in droves and congregate on deck, under a stretched tarpaulin. The number tops three hundred! I'm thrilled that Auntie Sally's daughter, Renee, who lives in London, is able to join me at this memorable event. She was born in Shanghai, after the war.

Color-coded ID cards, representing various camps, are handed out. Mine is pink. There are tears and shrieks of delight as, sixty years after WWII, fellow internees are reunited. Soon, other pink cardholders surround me. Media professionals and amateur photographers follow us around. They interview us, and record our animated chatter as we recount camp memories and speak about the Shanghai lilong—the lanes and alleys of our childhood.

The wavy-navy (reserves), in starched white uniforms, welcome guests with a parade and show of arms. Several octogenarian sailors from the original party happily reminisce with us, and appear to be as excited as we are!

Months earlier, BBC One, searching for ex-sailors, had sent out over 300 enquiries in a supreme, but vain effort to trace our own *Belfast* friend, Jimmy Corless, whose last known address was in Newcastle-Upon-Tyne. He had disappeared without a trace!

Caterers, weaving through the excited throng, deliver tray after tray of cream-topped jelly, sandwiches, buns, and finger foods, closely mimicking the 1945 party fare. Wine and tea are freely available.

Many "children" have brought precious memorabilia of photographs, copies of documents and drawings, and the degrading, mandatory, red and black numbered armbands worn by adults. We're recording our recollections verbally and on memory cards.

I'm rushing from corner to corner of the *Belfast*, reconnecting with people—basking blissfully in the sheer excitement of the day, and eating selected food offerings—"on the go."

Whenever I pass a particular group, one of the "children" sneers, "Every time I see you, you're feeding your face!"

Suddenly, I feel a stab of ancient pain well up. With a shock, I realize that sixty years later I am face to face with one of my childhood tormentors! I identify her when she, once again, manifests her inherent mean streak. There is no mistake!

I look her up and down slowly. Take in her chunky, frowsy appearance and her flat, ugly, brown farmhouse sandals. The styling and length of her lack-luster hair, ending just beneath her ears, suggesting it was executed with a bowl placed on her head as a guideline.

Ron Bridge carrying the flag at the cenotaph (closest person in photo).

"Yes," I say slowly, "and—aren't I lucky I can?"

Light rain is falling when, reluctantly, we leave with gift bags containing contact lists of the "children" at the party, videos, and various related items. At 9:30 that evening, the phone rings, and, half asleep, I end the day with a BBC telephone interview.

The following week I have two unexpected close encounters with royalty. The first is at a memorial attended by Prince Philip and other dignitaries, at the imposing Imperial War Museum. Then, on my last day in London, I wear my POW armband and join crowds of decorated veterans and distinguished guests at the Cenotaph. We watch Prince Charles lay a wreath at the 60th, and last, memorial service—in honor of the Japanese POWs who built the Burma Road.

# AUTHOR'S AFTERWORD

The Association of British Civilian Internees Far East Region (ABCIFER), was formed in London in January 1994. Its main purpose was to get an apology and claim restitution from Japan—$22,000 per civilian internee— for comprehensive losses during WWII. Most internees lost homes, possessions, financial assets, and documents. Many lost their education, pension rights, businesses, jobs, and insurance policies. Accordingly, they scattered to the four corners of the earth and had to start life anew—they lacked cohesion and had no voice.

Dedicated committee members worked tirelessly on our behalf. A tri-annual bulletin, *Bamboo Wireless*, kept us in touch and informed. Martyn Day, prominent lawyer of Leigh Day & Co of London, represented us, and with the help of Japanese lawyers, fought our case in Tokyo. The possibility of success stoked a great deal of hope. Unfortunately, despite meticulous preparation and tremendous effort, our lawyers were unsuccessful. Over twenty suits against the Japanese Government were initiated by different parties—among them the notorious *Comfort Women*. Japan claimed the 1951 San Francisco Peace Treaty settled all claims for restitution. It offered the weakest apology, blankly refusing to acknowledge culpability, and has concealed its unspeakably cruel war crimes from its own postwar generations.

In November 2000, Tony Blair, then Prime Minister, generated huge excitement when he announced a promise to make, as a "Debt of Honor," a single *ex-gratia* payment of £10,000 to "all who were British at the time of internment." He said, "It is very hard for someone of my generation to understand what suffering people went through. You saw the very worst of human nature, and yet I think you showed the very best of human nature. This is, for me and my generation and those younger, one small and significant way in which we can say 'thank you for your courage and thank you for what you did.'" The wording was unambiguous. Justice at last!

The UK War Pensions Agency, as the responsible authority, when asked in November 2000 what Tony Blair meant by being British, advised that the Cabinet Office had ruled that as long as you had a British passport on capture you were eligible. Then, after the May 2001 General Election, implementation was passed to the British Ministry of Defence (MoD), and Dr. Lewis Moonie, Armed Forces Minister at the time. In his Parliamentary comment Dr. Moonie said, unequivocally, "The Government recognizes that many UK citizens, both those serving in the armed forces and civilians, have had to endure great hardship at different times and in different circumstances, but the experience of those who went into captivity in the Far East during the second world war was unique. We have said before that we believe the country owes a debt of honor to them. I hope that I am speaking for everyone here when I say that today something concrete has been done to recognize that debt." Dr. Moonie also stated, "I guarantee absolutely that we shall consult all those involved to ensure that no one misses out on the payment... And they do not have to be living in Britain."

But by late May 2001, under the leadership of Dr. Moonie, the Ministry moved the goal posts and modified the *ex-gratia* definition by adding the words, "And who were born in the United Kingdom, or who had a parent or grandparent born in the United Kingdom." Our entire family, and many other ex-internees, were immediately excluded on the grounds that, lacking a direct ancestral "bloodlink" to the United Kingdom, we were "not British enough" to deserve payment of the *ex-gratia* "debt of honor."

When that was found illegal by the High Court, the Ministry, hedging, redefined being "British" in 1944 to mean living for 20 years post-1945 in England, and some other EU countries. The Ministry did not reclaim money from all those that had received payment before the change was effected—even though the recipients did not meet the new criteria. Countless letters and phone calls to relevant people in high office, including the Prime Minister, yielded negative results. I wrote: *After our release from internment in 1945, when repatriation of British and foreign nationals began, my father had gone repeatedly to the British authorities, requesting and pleading for our family's evacuation and safe passage. They refused us because we were not originally from the UK or Europe.*

In cold, courteous letters, consistently signed by a string of different people, the Ministry, despite being reminded of the Cabinet Office ruling of November 2000, resolutely continued to deny us equal rights as those with the deemed "correct ancestral bloodlink." It seemed any office passerby could sign the letters they dispatched so easily.

We felt violated! Where was British justice and fair play? How could the Ministry renege on its promise with impunity and perpetrate such a grave injustice? Their denial added insult to injury and mocked our past— by implying my family's hundreds of years of British nationality meant no more than just a passport, and blithely ignoring our lifelong financial deprivation and loss of optimum good health. I still remember my father standing so proudly at attention whenever the British National Anthem was played.

The Japanese asked no questions and made no distinctions—the sole reason for our incarceration was our British Nationality. ABCIFER's then Chairman, Ron Bridge, MBE AFC, represented us diligently, and fought ceaselessly on behalf of all those denied the ex-gratia payment, no matter where domiciled. He maintained constant contact and was unwaveringly supportive and informative.

After being denied the *ex-gratia* payment under the "birthlink" criterion, 81-year-old Mrs. Diana Elias challenged the redefinition of "British" and won her case in London, her post-war home for many years. She was awarded compensatory damages for injury to her feelings when discriminated against on the grounds of her national origins. The story was internationally publicized. Several similar "injury to feelings" claims followed. Unfavorable media reports frequently exposed the Ministry's negative response to our plight. Parliament had six debates. The three published Parliamentary Ombudsman's Reports found there had been at least four instances of "maladministration" over the affair and castigated those responsible and told them to rethink—all to no avail. The two Parliamentary Select Committee inquiries and reports found the UK Ministry of Defence to blame, but to date the MoD have swept those reports under the table, totally ignoring them.

Finally, thanks to all the adverse publicity steadily chipping away at the Ministry, a small measure of success was achieved. We received two token payments; the first in 2006, £500 as an "apology for injured feelings," and then, in October 2007, after signing a mandatory agreement to waive all future claims, we received a second payment of US$7,320.

While welcome, the money we received could never compensate for the years of pain and stress caused by our ongoing battle for justice. Many deserving recipients, including my father and brother, died before the inadequate token payments were disbursed. It was estimated that, out of the 19,500 British civilians incarcerated in WWII, 3000 were still alive, and 2980 applied for the so-called ex-gratia. 1400 were paid in the first few months, then, after the High Court battles, another 1000 were paid, some 500 received the reduced sum, and about 50 are still waiting. This was a clear example of a Government's duplicity and politicians wriggling.

Ultimately, vacillating probably cost the Ministry more than if it had honored its original promise to pay, equally, "all who were British at the time of internment." As well, it could have avoided muddying its name and reputation by all the adverse publicity. I hope it will someday have the courage and decency to admit committing what was widely perceived to be a travesty of honest British justice, and make a long overdue, genuine apology to us. We are truly counted among the ones that proudly held the British far-eastern fort, and, in doing so lost so much.

# ACKNOWLEDGEMENTS

In 1987, after my father suffered a serious bout of pneumonia, I armed myself with a recorder and taped the first of three interviews of both parents over a 23-year period. I could not have written my manuscript without their invaluable generous input, for which I thank them.

I am deeply grateful to my Australian cousins Michael and Leanne Minny, who dedicated long hours reading, assembling, compiling and binding my first draft; Hazel Minny Campbell, Ed Minny, David Rubain, and my aunt, Eileen Feller, filled in many gaps with shared stories, photographs and memorabilia. Heartfelt thanks to my Canadian cousins, Miriam Abrahams and Doreen Affleck, for reading my manuscript and enriching my story with invaluable input, and furnishing me with the incredible ancestral photographs that I had no idea existed.

Thank you all fellow internees who generously supplied bits of memorabilia that jogged my memory and enriched my manuscript—in particular, author Margaret Blair, (*Gudao, Lone Islet*), Dick Germaine, for sending a copy of *Camp Chit-Chat*, and Abe Abraham for sharing his camp stories.

Nelson Oliver kindly furnished multiple archived Vancouver BC newspaper articles about the *Empress of Asia* that evacuated nationals to Hong Kong during the battle for Shanghai in 1937.

For several years I had the good fortune to be part of an incredible critique group that greatly enhanced my writing. Thank you so much to authors Diana Johnson, Howard Goldstein and Dolly Wise, for your unstinting input and encouragement.

For valuable suggestions and constant support I thank my dear friends David and Sonia Hoffman—Sonia painstakingly read and constructively critiqued my manuscript. I owe a special debt of gratitude to my friends Elaine and Gil Skopp—Gil meticulously and caringly edited my book and was always available to help me over my "humps."

There are no words to describe my indebtedness to Scott Greene for magically repairing and restoring my images, and formatting my manuscript. His creative genius breathed life into my cover design.

Special thanks to all my family and friends for their constant support and various degrees of involvement, and, for reading, input and unflagging encouragement: award winning authors and producers Lionel and Diana Friedberg, authors Jana McBurney-Lin (*My Half of the Sky*), Larry Engelmann (*Daughter of China*), and Corinne Copnick (*Cryo Kid*); Stan and Karon Shear, Frank and Blossom Chen, Tammy Bloomfield, Dr. Jack Share, Eric Lieberman, and Dr. Ron Lever for snapping my back cover photo.

My measureless gratitude to Ron Bridge, MBE AFC, chairman of ABCIFER, (Association of British Civilian Internees Far East Region) for his tireless fights on our behalf to receive compensation from the Japanese, and the ex-gratia payment from the British Ministry of Defence (MoD), denied us when they decided we were "not British enough" to qualify. Born in Tientsin (now Tianjin) he was interned for three years in Weihsien Camp. His grandparents had gone to China in the 1880s, and his paternal grandfather was one of the few Englishmen who were made Mandarins by the Empress Dowager.

Use of IWM image number A30855—me swinging on the *HMS Belfast*—was made possible by generous written permission from Yvonne Oliver of the Imperial War Museum in London, where, twice in 2005, I was warmly welcomed and afforded an extensive opportunity to relate my story.

Meghan Spillane, Community Development Manager of King George V School in Hong Kong, graciously granted permission to use references and archived photographs of my childhood school.

Many thanks to the composer (possibly Agnes Baden-Powell) of the song; *We're the Girl Guides Marching on the King's Highway*. I have faithfully applied due diligence in my unsuccessful attempt to locate the source and year of publication of a song that has been meaningful to Guides worldwide.

I salute authors Iris Chang (*The Rape of Nanking*), Hanchao Lu (*Beyond the Neon Lights*), David Kranzler (*Japanese, Nazis & Jews*), Stella Dong (*Shanghai*), and numerous other authors for the incredible insight and information I gleaned from their books. They kept my memories alive and heightened my enthusiasm for completing my manuscript.

Made in the USA
Charleston, SC
18 December 2012